The
Deeds
of
Christ

The
Deeds
of
Christ

HAROLD A. BOSLEY

🄯 ABINGDON PRESS
NASHVILLE AND NEW YORK

THE DEEDS OF CHRIST

Copyright © 1969 by Abingdon Press

Library of Congress Catalog Card Number: 69-12017

Scripture quotations unless otherwise noted are
from the Revised Standard Version of the Bible,
copyrighted 1946 and 1952 by the Division of
Christian Education, National Council of
Churches, and are used by permission.

The material in Chapter 9, Section II, pp. 135-39,
is revised from Dr. Bosley's book A Firm Faith for
Today, published by Harper & Brothers, © 1950.

SET UP, PRINTED, AND BOUND BY THE
PARTHENON PRESS, AT NASHVILLE,
TENNESSEE, UNITED STATES OF AMERICA

*To the oncoming generation
of churchmen in*
Christ Church (United Methodist)
New York City

Contents

Introduction

We live in the day of the Deed. Unless a word is incarnate in a person or an act or a policy, it is without meaning that commands attention. Necessarily, we have developed a philosophy of sorts to rationalize the Deed—existentialism, we call it. We have little or no interest in still life in art or in the dissection of life by analysts. We want the whole of the moment, the event, the action, the person. Traditional philosophies and theologies that stress the ideal, the essence, or the form as being of basic importance continue to speak, but few listen to what they may be saying.

Sheer dynamism is one of the tokens of our day. Jack Kerouac has caught this spirit in his book *On the Road*, particularly in an interchange between two of his characters. One says, "We gotta go and never stop till we get there." "Where we going, man?" asks the other. "I don't know, but we gotta go" is the answer. This is one of the most poignant and appealing aspects of the life of the younger generations now. They are on the move; they are going places—to the Peace Corps, to the moon, to Washington to demonstrate. They are no spectator generation; they are not even a listening generation, when it comes to paying much attention to the deluge of advice their fathers keep pouring in their general direction. They are more determined to be heard than they are to hear, a fact which accelerates the already high blood pressure of their fathers. The courageous, even bellicose, protest movements on and off campuses tell their own story, and I may as well admit that I find it a most encouraging one. I deny that we of the older generation have much moral right to advise them on very many things. And if we attempt to, I know of no reason why they should do more than genuflect slightly out of respect for age and effort. Our mistakes have lighted fires all over the world. Every continent is ablaze with our stupidities and our sins. They threaten to discredit the many great achievements we may claim. Words alone cannot put them out; only the Deed has a chance of doing that. The Deed is life; the Word (any word) without the Deed is death—even when it speaks of life.

This, I suggest, is the reason why we in the Christian tradition must pay renewed attention to the Deed of God in Jesus Christ and his incredible hope that we should become the Deed incarnate in his name. Even as he was a man of action in the name and for the sake of God, so must his followers come alive in similar fashion. We must understand him as a real human being who lived among human beings and sought to lead them out of the poverty of their lives into the fullness of God's will for them. In Paul's probing word: "God was in

Christ reconciling the world to himself, . . . and entrusting to us the message of reconciliation."

The purpose of this book is to see Jesus Christ in certain areas of significant action; to catch something of the incarnate purpose of his life; to sense the vigor, the determination, and the unfailing compassion of that life. Without in the least trying to identify Bonhoeffer with what follows, I have a feeling that he would understand what I am trying to do and would approve it, even though he would surely do it in his own way and much better.

This book is the third in the series dealing with Jesus Christ, the earlier ones being *The Mind of Christ* and *The Character of Christ*. All three—and other meditations in the series of which they were a part—were shared with the people committed to my care in Christ Church Methodist of New York City. Having dedicated the preceding book to the faithful congregation of that church, I dedicate this one to the oncoming generation of churchmen, who even now are moving into positions of leadership in our life and work.

HAROLD A. BOSLEY

11

1. He Lived Among Us

Scripture: *Luke 2:21-52*

Text: *Jesus increased in wisdom and in stature, and in favor with God and man.*

I

Shortly before his imprisonment and eventual execution, Dietrich Bonhoeffer wrote the substance of his most significant book, *Ethics*. Imbedded in it is a paragraph which better than anything else explains his faith and thought:

In Soloviev's story of the Antichrist, in the last days before Christ's return the heads of the persecuted churches discuss the question of what is for each of them the most precious thing in Christianity; *the decisive answer is that the most precious thing in Christianity is Jesus Christ Himself. . . .* Only he who shares in Him has the power to withstand and to overcome. He is the centre and the strength of the Bible, of the Church, and of theology, but also of humanity, of reason, of justice and of culture. Everything must return to Him; it is only under His protection that it can live.[1]

We shall be attempting to return to Jesus Christ through a study of his deeds; not all of them, as recorded in the Gospels, but those that enable us to see deeply into the workings of his mind and spirit. We today are uniquely able to do this, for ours is the age of the doer, the man who gets things done. Other ages have exalted man the thinker, man the mystic, man the warrior. But we prostrate ourselves before man the doer. If Rodin's most famous bronze celebrates man the thinker, then the magnificent figure on the state capitol at Lincoln, Nebraska, celebrates man the doer. For it is a depiction of the sower—the man who went forth to sow!

The appreciation of deeds has a long rootage in the American experience. Emerson, staid idealist and philosopher of a century ago, admired men of action even though he scarcely qualified as one himself. One morning he was trying to shove a balky calf into a barn. They were having quite a tussle of it when the unlettered hired man who had been milking the cows came out of the barn, took in the situation with a glance, went back into the barn, wet his finger in some milk, and came out and put his finger in the calf's mouth; the calf followed him eagerly into the barn. Emerson looked at the retreating calf for a moment, then retired to his study and wrote,

[1] Eberhard Bethge, ed. (New York: The Macmillan Co., 1965), p. 178 (italics mine).

14

"I like men who get things done." And so do we all!

Our Lord himself preferred men of deeds to men of words. Recall, if you will, the fact that he wanted no part of those who fawned upon him, saying, "Lord, Lord," yet would not do what he said. He turned to those who obeyed without making a public show of it. He is the author of the oldest-known statement of the basic principle of pragmatism, the philosophy of action: "You will know them by their fruits." And the deed is the full-grown fruit of desire, intention, and purpose. Until an ideal, however noble, is objectified and incarnated in a deed, it remains intradermal, unreal, ephemeral. Describe it any way we will, it does not count in the coin of human living unless it comes alive in a deed.

What we shall be attempting in this series of studies is to begin with the deeds chronicled in the Gospels and then travel back, as we are able, to motive, intention, and spirit, hoping to get better acquainted with the whole person who lies back of and is revealed in the deed. We will begin in, continue with, and be guided by the Gospel records, for the Four Gospels tell us 99.9 percent of all we know or claim to know about the life and teachings of Jesus Christ. We do have some fragments of many early gospels other than the four in the New Testament, but without exception they seem to be products of the unfettered imaginations of devout souls who lived much later than the first century.

Then too, the Four Gospels plus the book of Acts are the only parts of the New Testament that seem to be seriously interested in the earthly life of our Lord. We can read all the New Testament that follows the book of Acts and find only two or three clear references to his life and teachings. The epistles in the New Testament suggest that the Christian groups described therein were well acquainted with the stories of him, thanks to the travels of men like Peter. The latter part of the New Testament is set to a different task: to explore the fuller meanings of Jesus Christ. But it seldom attempts to go back to any given deed or teaching and enlarge upon it. Paul in his letters to the Corinthians cites the story of what Jesus did and said at the Last Supper with the disciples. His quote in Acts is the sole source of Jesus' word, "It is more blessed to give than to receive." But Paul pays no attention to the infancy stories that were circulating in the early churches and little more to the detailed accounts of the crucifixion and the resurrection, though he was infinitely more interested in this than in any other part of the life of our Lord.

"Why," we ask, "do New Testament writers pay so little attention to the earthly life of Jesus Christ?" The answer, to put it briefly, is that they assumed the reality of that life and probed for its eternal meaning. They believed that they lived at the end of one age and were soon to be led into another by the risen and eternal Christ. Why, then, be concerned about how he lived from day to day—his home, work, clothing, companions, etc.,—when the *point* and the *significance* of his life lay elsewhere, namely in preparation for the age to come?

The otherworldly emphasis of the early church lies on every page of the New Testament, and we do its writers a grave injustice if we make light of it. Mark and Luke seem concerned about it, for they sought to keep the new faith closely tied in with life, but even they finally awaited the return of Jesus in glory to judge the living and the dead.

The most radical difference between New Testament times and our own lies precisely here. The otherworldly emphasis of the early faith is wholly foreign to most of us. I doubt whether one in ten thousand confessing Christians today actually and honestly expects Jesus Christ to return to the earth in any form at any time actually to judge all men, living and dead. Nor would any large number play down the importance of our day-to-day life on this earth; it is of ultimate, not transitory, importance, we think. We are not waiting for the end of one age and the beginning of another. As far as we are concerned, *"This is it!"* There may be—and we faithfully believe there is—a life beyond this one, but not for a moment do we think of separating the two.

It is the recovery of the sense of the ultimate importance of life and work that causes us to renew and deepen our knowledge of the life and work of Jesus Christ. We want to get acquainted with him as a man among men, as one who actually lived among people like us on this earth.

Some eminent scholars—not all by any means—will warn that we are on a risky journey. They call attention to the scanty nature of our records and to the bias with which they were written. Yet we must not desist because of such difficulties—unless we propose to give up

17

Jesus Christ as the center of our faith. We ought to be as faithful as the novelist Sholem Asch and many others who attempt with painstaking care to reconstruct the pattern of the life in which Jesus shared. We believe not only in the historicity of Jesus—that he actually lived on this earth—but we believe most devoutly in his humanity as well as in what, for lack of a better term, we call his divinity.

Every attempt at biography must begin with the antecedents of the person under study and then proceed to sketch the main lines of his growth to manhood. Having done this, we are ready for an account and appraisal of the main moments in his mature life and an evaluation of them. This is the general pattern we shall be following in this study.

II

Jesus was born in the country of Palestine, in the little village of Bethlehem, five miles south of Jerusalem. Bethlehem was a fabled village in Hebrew lore, for in or near it David grew to manhood. Jesus' parents were of the lineage of David and were in Bethlehem at the time of Jesus' birth, obeying a Roman order which required the registration of all Jews in the city of their birth. They seem not to have lingered long in Bethlehem. As soon as Mary was able to travel, they left, going according to Matthew to Egypt but according to Luke to Nazareth, the only earthly home Jesus knew and the village where he lived all but the last three years of his life.

Of those early years we know next to nothing of his actual life. Only one event breaks through the surface of those "hidden years," as far as the Gospel records are concerned—the well-known trip to Jerusalem for the Passover when he was twelve years of age. Like most boys of that age he had a perfect penchant for worrying his parents by getting lost in a great crowd. No parent will find that story hard to understand!

Several early manuscripts called the Infancy Gospels try to fill in the hidden years with more detail, but they are better understood as poetic expressions of a human desire to picture what he might have done than as carefully weighed and reasonably trustworthy stories about his boyhood. The early church treasured them along with hundreds of other such efforts but flatly refused to rank them with the Gospels as trustworthy interpretations of his life.

Yet this lack of direct evidence about the day-to-day events in his early life does not add up to no trustworthy knowledge at all. The veil over the hidden years has been lifted in many ways by careful scholarship, and we are now able to piece together a reasonably complete picture of where and how he lived and of the events that swept like tidal waves through his early life.

We know that he lived in the household of a carpenter and probably in later boyhood became the main support of a family left without a head by Joseph's death. Carpentering was one of the honorable and essential crafts of that day. A good carpenter was as important to the Nazareth of Jesus' day as, say, a blacksmith was to the farm community in which many of us grew up, or a good mechanic is to our motorized age.

The Italian novelist Giovanni Papini went so far as to write, "The husbandman, the blacksmith, the mason, and the carpenter are the workmen whose art is most intimately bound up with human life; theirs are the best and most truly religious of occupations." [2]

Jesus grew up in a carpenter's home and learned to work with every kind of building material then in use: wood, stone, rock, metal, and the mixture of dirt and sand which was the roofing material for homes. There were no wholesalers! Each carpenter shop had to get its own materials from the woods and the quarries and have them on hand in sufficient supply. We do not know where Joseph and his sons went for wood; there were large forests east, north, and south of Nazareth, along the Jordan, and around the wells and oases.

This recalls to me an incident from my boyhood: the time in the fall when we would "make the winter's wood," as my father described it. He would buy a piece of "standing timber" near our home, and we had to get it down, sawed and chopped into usable sizes. I am sure Joseph and his sons enjoyed their wood-gathering expeditions. And the trips to nearby quarries for various kinds of stone and other building materials took the boys into the cave regions of Galilee and may have taken

[2] Quoted in Henri Daniel-Rops, *Jesus and His Times* (New York: E. P. Dutton & Co., 1966), p. 150.

20

them to the nearest port city where the Romans were unloading materials for the building of several beautiful cities in that area.

Once the raw material was stacked outside the wall of the little shop in Nazareth, then came the arduous task of shaping it by means of saw and adz, chisel and hammer —a seemingly endless task to a boy who wanted to play! The slabs of stone piled outside the home would need continual attention too, as buyers would want them for special purposes. Caravan masters would want casks —barrels, we call them—made and fitted in rope slings for use by camel and ass or on shipboard when the caravans reached port. While much of the storing of fruit and oil was in jars—easily the best way—some must have been in casks made in a hundred little carpenter shops scattered throughout the country.

While most building of homes was done on a do-it-yourself plan, then, as now, an expert carpenter would be needed for much of the work. Beds and alcoves needed to be built; stools and benches were wanted for rooftops; patios or outside gardens, however small, were needed; threshing floors for winnowing the grain were essential in the life of every family; bowls for use in the kitchens were always in short supply, and hewing them out must have been a task that a boy could do under his father's watchful eye.

Undoubtedly, then as now, devout men turned their hands gladly to the building and servicing of a house or place of worship. There was a synagogue in Nazareth, and Joseph and his sons had surely shared in building and maintaining it. Some carpenters and stone masons became excellent artists as the few wood and stone carvings we have from that day attest. And in an earlier century Isaiah had lashed out at the carpenters who made wooden idols for people to have in their houses! But not Joseph and his sons, we may be sure. I am confident that they had put their hands to either or both the building or the repairing of the very synagogue in which Jesus preached his first sermon following his call to the public ministry.

His life in Nazareth—indeed, his entire life—was one of extraordinary simplicity. A thoroughly competent scholar sums it up this way: "Jesus led the ordinary life of poor people of his time. He lived in a humble home . . . ate the common food of the Galilean people: barley bread, very little meat, vegetables and sour milk, and on feast days grilled fish." [3]

G. A. Studdert-Kennedy's poem "It's Hard to Be a Carpenter" catches the harmonies of all this in a moving way:

> I wonder what He charged for chairs at Nazareth.
> And did men try to beat Him down, . . .
> And did they promise and not pay,
> Put it off to another day, . . .
> I wonder did He have bad debts,
> And did He know my fears and frets?

[3] *Ibid.*

22

> The Gospel writer here forgets
> To tell about the Carpenter.
> But that's just what I want to know.
> Ah! Christ in glory, here below
> Men cheat and lie to one another so
> It's hard to be a carpenter.[4]

The word "poor" is hardly accurate in describing the home of Jesus. Few Galileans were wealthy even by Roman standards, but there is no reason to believe that the level of living in Joseph's home was below that of other artisans in Nazareth. Jesus' playmates, associates, fellow workers, and, later, disciples, came from the ranks of ordinary or common people—the fishermen, artisans, and laborers in the fields—and from the marshalling points of the caravans. He lived their life; he spoke their language; he discussed the same issues and events for the thirty years he lived in Nazareth; he knew them best; he had complete confidence in them.

It is a misnomer to call these "the hidden years"; they were the formative years for him. They were the years when he walked the roadways of life as any other human being, a man among men; the years when the later creedal word was fact, "and was made man." Small wonder he knew what was in man and could speak so directly to the human heart!

[4] Abridgment of "It's Hard to Be a Carpenter" by G. A. Studdert-Kennedy from *The Best of Studdert-Kennedy* (Harper, 1929). Used by permission of Harper & Row and Hodder and Stoughton, Ltd.

III

We cannot read the records of his life—fragmentary and in some cases quite unsatisfactory, though they are —without being impressed with the believability of most of the people he dealt with. His family—Mary and his brothers and sisters—were not paper saints. They were worried about him and his safety—even his sanity, when the first reports of his public ministry came to them. They did what worried relatives have done from time immemorial: they tried to get him to come home and give up his mad dream. But when he would not, they stuck with him to the very end, just as relatives usually do. His family never let him down, even when they were not quite sure of what he was about. And his mother both saw him die and was on hand to prepare his body for burial.

When I think of the holy family, I do not think of Jesus, Mary, and Joseph alone; I think of the entire family that lived, laughed, worked, worried, suffered, and mourned together throughout his lifetime. Even though he did not marry, as most young men did, he knew the meaning of family life and responsibility and gained from them his profound confidence in love, compassion, and forgiveness.

His neighbors were everyman's neighbors. We know none of them by name and seldom see them in a specific way in the Gospels. Like typical neighbors they just could not believe it when word came that he had taken to preaching the gospel of the kingdom of God and people were talking of him as Messiah! He, Messiah? He was Jesus, son of Joseph and Mary, with several brothers and two sisters right down the street, he could not be the Messiah, the long-awaited deliverer of Israel! They could not and they did not believe it. When he returned to Nazareth for his first sermon in the synagogue, he probably knew the name and family of every person in the sanctuary. Taking advantage of this, he chided them sharply for doubting that he had been called of God to proclaim the message of the Messiah. And they, indignant as only neighbors can be, were all for throwing him out of town forthwith. But he spared them the trouble by leaving of his own accord, settling in Capernaum, a city some miles to the east, and using it as the seat of his public ministry.

He lived among wavering disciples too. They wanted so much to believe and to keep faith. But he kept asking the impossible of them. Try as they might, they could not keep pace with his demanding spirit. But they tried and kept on trying until by the grace of God they took the torch from his falling hands and held it high as long as they lived. That is, all but one did. And thanks to this one, Jesus knew the meaning of, felt the impossible tragedy of, betrayal by a friend, a trusted disciple.

He faced the indignation of what we would call the power structure in the religious life of his people—the priests, rabbis, and students of the law, the lawyers. He who knew scripture as well as they, found himself in a scripture-matching contest with them time and again. He heard them quote scripture to discredit, if not condemn, him and even the kingdom of God! He heard them charge him with violating the sabbath, profaning the temple, breaking moral conventions, speaking disrespectfully to the high priests, and repeatedly showing less than proper respect for the Pharisees, the widely acknowledged exemplars of true faith.

Candidly, there was much truth in such charges. When he felt that the religious leaders stood between man and God, that they were perverting scripture to serve their own purposes, that they hid ethical injustices beneath their robes of piety, he said so in words that still quiver with indignation. He meant it when he cried, "Woe to you, scribes and Pharisees, hypocrites!"

He knew and loved the multitudes, but he never thought of them as the multitudes. They were always individual human beings to him. Some were so badly in debt that they were forced to steal to live; others were driven to the wall by angry creditors. Some workers were exploited by ruthless masters, but some were evil enough to steal from their master and even to kill his son when they had an opportunity to do so. He knew men as hungry, thirsty, needy people whose loved ones sickened and died, whose children ran away from home, and who themselves fell into evil ways. How it must have hurt him when the ones he knew best and reached out to most eagerly—the multitudes—either turned away from him in apathy or turned on him in anger!

So he had no illusions about the multitudes, collectively or individually. He had become acquainted with their strengths and weaknesses over thirty years of living among them. Consequently, he was prepared for the reactions of village elders across the Sea of Galilee who were startled by his cure of the man with the demons and stunned by the loss of their pigs. And finally it was the loss of their pigs that meant the most to them. So much so that they asked him to leave the country! He was invited out of more places in Palestine in the three years of his public ministry than anyone else we have any record of! It's hard to take that in as a fact, isn't it? That anyone would actually ask Jesus Christ to move on! But the record is clear that that is precisely what happened time and time again.

He lived among confessing sinners as well as professing saints. And he did so without condescension; he took them to be children of God. Mary Magdalene was a notorious prostitute; Zacchaeus was an infamous tax gatherer, but the word soon got out among their kind that here was a man who welcomed them, who talked with them, who seemed to believe in them and urged them to believe that God was actually holding open the door to a new and better life for all of them, no matter who they were or what they had done. Of course they flocked around him in life and in death alike!

IV

Our awareness, then, of the true meaning of Jesus Christ begins with his humanity, with the fact that he lived among us as one of us, that, as the book of Hebrews puts it, he was "in every respect . . . tempted as we are, yet without sinning." He became a moving force among men because he knew what was in man. He can reach us today because he knows who and what we are. He has stood where we stand. He—of whom we say we either take his way or choose disaster—became a decisive force in history because he was intimately acquainted with the stuff of history: human beings living together for better or for worse. He became the ethical and moral power par excellence because he understood why we do what we do. To stand before him is to stand before a spiritual fluoroscope wherein we see what goes on inside our spiritual being. He lived in a war-ravaged country, yet felt within it God's call to peace. He lived among a people whose majestic religious heritage was losing its world vision and becoming a cult, yet found within it a way of life and strength for living that have nourished men of all times and all places.

The crowning realization is this: somewhere along that journey of thirty years—probably all along it—he learned of God and found him in ordinary daily events and ordinary human relationships. To be sure, he had learned of God in scripture and solemn religious service, but he felt the impulse of God's will wherever he turned. How open, indescribably, sensitively open, he must have been to all things! No trudging through life like "the man with the hoe" with "the light blown out within his brain"! How eagerly and actively he must have searched the depths of every day for new evidences of God's love and mercy. He found them too, and because he found them, we know they are there and know how to look for them, provided we are willing to pay the price of discipleship.

John sums it up perfectly in his wonderful word, "The Word became flesh and dwelt among us, full of grace and truth; we have beheld his glory, glory as of the only Son from the Father. . . . And from his fullness have we all received, grace upon grace."

2. He Found God in Life

Scripture: *Luke 2:21-52*

Text: *Jesus increased in wisdom and in stature, and in favor with God and man.*

I

Most of us were jarred at least for a moment by two quite unrelated events. One was the flip statement by the first Russian cosmonaut when he returned from his brief excursion into outer space to the effect that he did not see God there. I doubt whether he really expected to see God there or anywhere else! I doubt too whether he knew what he was looking for—if, perchance, he was actually looking for God. Most reasonably literate persons know that we will never travel far enough into outer space to find God there; nor, for that matter, far enough into inner space to find him there. We just do not find God like we find a place on a map or an organ within our bodies and say, "Here God is."

The second jolt came with the clamorous insistence of two death-of-God theologians—Hamilton and Altizer —that they find ultimate meaning in Jesus Christ but not in God. This, to me, is an incredible and utterly indefensible posture, misrepresenting both Christ and God. It is simply impossible to separate Jesus Christ from his own personal awareness of and loving obedience to God. His awareness of God's love, his knowledge of God's claim on him, his steady reliance on God each step of the way—in the wilderness as his ministry began and in the garden as it ended—these, I say, are the literal center of his life and teachings. Take them out, and his meaning collapses into a self-deceived person who nourished himself on some impossible myth about God. Jesus Christ and God are inseparable, as far as the records go. He was keenly and sensitively aware of God and attuned to his every movement in life. For he had found God in life.

That is the fact we want to examine in some detail now, for it explains not only the deeds of Jesus Christ, but also the historic Christian claim that *Jesus Christ is himself the great deed of God.*

II

Jesus of Nazareth was born into and nurtured by one of the most intensive and intelligent religious traditions known to man. When it threw its mantle over him 2,000 years ago, it was already ancient and well tested through at least 1,500 years of human experience. It was this-worldly in the exact sense that it spoke of human beings, about human problems, and about a proper relationship to God and among men. It was other-worldly too, but in the equally exact sense that it spoke of God, his covenant with men in the law, and held before men the realistic and relevant hopes of being a holy people living in a holy land under the guidance of a holy law.

From earliest beginnings Hebrew religion was rooted in life and deeply sensitive to all that went on in the depths of life. It was concerned about events in the lives of people who lived in Ur of the Chaldees, in Egypt, and in the wilderness, as well as in the Holy Land. It centered its stories in men like Abraham, Isaac, Jacob, Moses, David, and the prophets. It described the way God worked with these men in and through the events that gave their lives eternal meaning.

God called Abraham from Ur of the Chaldees and sent him on his life of ceaseless wandering. God sent the sons of Judah to Egypt, where one rose to glory under the pharaohs. God called Moses from the security of his life as a shepherd to the dangerous post of leading the Israelites from slavery into freedom. God raised up David, the shepherd boy, and made him king of Israel, sustaining him when he was obedient and punishing him when he was not. When God wanted a fresh word spoken to his people, he singled out Isaiah in the temple or Jeremiah or Amos or Micah, as each went about his ordinary course of living.

God gave the Israelites a law to follow as obedient children. It covered the whole range of daily problems and human relationships. It dealt with an amazingly comprehensive list of things to be done and not done. It exalted the altar and the temple as places where men should come with the appropriate sacrifices composed of the fruits of their fields and flocks. It laid out the life of the priest with meticulous detail as to clothing, food, and drink. Yet it was equally concerned to lay out the proper way of dealing with slaves or employees; it was most explicit on the position and duties of father, mother, and children in the home and the community.

The religious tradition which was a part of the life of Jesus of Nazareth was itself a part of the life of his people over many centuries. And it was alive from beginning to end with the deeds of God in history and in the lives of the people who make up history.

I emphasize the word "deeds" because we so easily fall into the habit of thinking of religion as being primarily concerned with mystical visions and mysterious events. While there were mystical visions aplenty in this religious tradition, the warp and woof of it were something quite different; they were the calm, almost detached recitals of what God said and did and of how men responded to God's approach and God's commands. But the creative moments, the pivotal ones, always see God relating himself to man in history at a given place and time through some need that is clamoring for a new answer.

Moses is the central figure in the first five books of

33

the Bible. Jesus had been nurtured on the stories of Moses: Moses as a castaway child, the adopted son of Pharaoh's household, the slayer of a man, a fugitive from justice, a shepherd in an out-of-the-way oasis in the desert, an unwilling and apprehensive deliverer of his people from slavery, an even more anxious and apprehensive traveler up Mt. Sinai to receive the Law, an angry leader when he saw the golden calf, and a man who was permitted to guide his people to the banks of the Jordan—but no farther. Small wonder, then, that the law of Moses was also a law of life and a law for living, for it was struck up and out of real life itself, and it answered to concrete needs that human beings faced as they sought to know and to obey the God of their fathers.

This was the law Jesus studied as a boy in the synagogue school. And as long as Joseph lived, he fulfilled his duty as a father in Israel by teaching his family in the reading or recital of the Law, especially in the stories of Moses. With Joseph's early death Jesus as the eldest son undoubtedly assumed this same responsibility when he was able to do so. It is an interesting thought, isn't it, that long before he was called by God into the public ministry, he had taught or interpreted the Law to the little family in whose life he shared?

But the part of his heritage closest to him revolved around David, for he was of the lineage of David. The family of the carpenter might be artisans, but the blood of kings flowed in their veins. I am sure of this fact added a dimension of warmth to the psalms which they recited daily, for the psalms were attributed to David, the sweet singer of Israel. David was more than a king and a singer; he was a warrior. He and his armies had fought many of their battles in the near neighborhood of Nazareth, and the very hillsides over which Jesus and his comrades played were storied with the deeds of David. The annual journeys to Jerusalem for the great festivals undoubtedly included side trips to Bethlehem, their ancestral home a few miles to the south.

Yet David could never be just one among many ancestors to them. He was a man of God; one raised up by God to throw off the yoke of oppression, to build the Holy City, to bring the ark into it, and to make of it the central shrine in their lives. Once the ark containing the broken tablets of the Law had come to rest on the highest mountain in that area, the little village round about it became the Holy City.

Even so, David knew the displeasure of God time after time because he would not obey him. Because he was a warrior, a man of blood, God deemed him unfit to build the temple. That was reserved for his son Solomon. Because he was guilty of adultery, his family split apart; one son rebelled against him and was slain, and David was well-nigh inconsolable in his grief. But after a period of violent grief he was told by God in no uncertain terms to be up and about his work once more in the service of God!

Jesus of Nazareth learned of the hardness of life from his tradition. For in it there were drought, famine, earthquake, and war. There were slavery, exile, and the slow, agonizing rebuildings of life, temple, and city time after time. There were the recitals of man's inhumanity to man—so great that God raised up Micah, Amos, Hosea, and the prophets to rebuke it and Assyria, Babylon, and Egypt to punish it. Life could get hard, very hard indeed, for those who incurred the displeasure of God through disobedience. Jesus grasped in this the firmness and the dependability of God. The God who spoke to him from sacred tradition was one whose will was conveyed by the Law and who insisted on that Law, yet whose will far transcended the Law at any given time.

The tradition of prophecy must have had a special appeal to Jesus—at least most of his references to scripture are to some prophetic book or other. The religion of the Hebrews was too close to life to be tied down to any set of laws. The dynamic power of life itself demanded fresh utterance in new situations. That is where the prophets came in, not to set aside the Law, but to supplement it, to interpret anew with a fresh vision, a new word, God's will for his people . Jesus must have puzzled over the collisions between priest and prophet which dot the pages of the history of his people. The priest, tied to a literal interpretation of the Law and a literal celebration of its ceremonies, was dead set against the prophet who pleaded in behalf of a new vision which God had given him for the life of his people.

It was this tradition—"expectation" is a better word —of a new vision that kept Israel on the spiritual toes of expectancy through the centuries. For slowly but surely the hope of a Messiah, a deliverer, one raised up and empowered by God to cast off oppression and to restore the kingdom of David, took form and became a power in their thought, their prayers, and their life. Men believed that this would actually happen. Each time a new voice of prophecy was raised, men would ask, "Could this be the Messiah?" Four times—perhaps more often—within the lifetime of Jesus that cry was raised and the new messiahs rallied their warriors for a fanatical assault on the Roman legions—only to die in their own blood. Clearly, it was a dangerous thing to be, or to be known as, the Messiah. And with equal clarity, it came home to our Lord that the Messiah who would be sent of God was quite different from the messiahs men had been wanting and welcoming.

Just how dangerous, he could not have known until his own people rejected both his radical reinterpretation of the work of a Messiah and him along with it. They not so much let as asked that he be put to death on a Roman cross as the deceiver of their hopes and their dreams.

III

What manner of being was it Jesus found when he found God in life? Not wholly unlike the God of his fathers, to be sure. In fact, he was very like the Lord described in Isaiah (Chapters 40–55) and many of the psalms. But when all is said about how much Jesus "borrowed" from the faith of his fathers, the fact remains that taken all in all, he brought a fresh word about God and became known himself as God's word of life to men.

The God whom he found in life was for him as for

37

his fathers, the Lord of life. He was, and is, the One whom men know as Creator, Sustainer, and Redeemer. He holds all life in the hollow of his hand. He is firm, purposive, and loving in his dealing with all creation. Yet his ways are past finding out, and men must learn to live by faith when they are in the presence of the deeds of God that pass their understanding or their ability to interpret them in the light of their own experiences. For time after time Jesus, as well as his ancestors, was led into a situation where he had to walk by faith rather than by sight in his obedience to God, the Lord of life.

The God whom he found in life was one whose will and love embraced all men, including Israel. While his fathers might have wanted to limit the love of God to Israel, this would not do for the God whom Jesus found in life. For in his sight all men are precious; all are his children; all are the objects of his ministrations in nature, history, and personal experience. There is nothing in Jesus' thought that would limit God in time, in place, or to a certain people.

The God whom he found in life is one whose compassion, whose loving concern, outranges anything men had ever dreamed of or anything we can know or imagine. Ask Jesus how it is possible for God to love all men, and he would surely reply that even as it is possible for rain and sun to fall upon all men, the love of God can come to all. And God's love is personal and firm. God never gives up on anyone—no matter who he is or what he has done. All men are God's children. Let someone bargain away her virtue and seemingly sink below the level of

38

any form of decency; she nonetheless is still one who can hear—if she will listen—the saving word, "Neither do I condemn you; go, and do not sin again."

The God whom he found in life was one whose love was as wide and deep—yes, wider and deeper—than life itself. No law could limit that love or its ministrations to men. No rite or ceremony could contain it. No religious establishment, be it temple, synagogue, or church, could claim to control it. Being of God's essence, his love is as infinite as he is. And since it is love, it is his unfailing compassion toward all men.

The God Jesus found in life was the Lord of suffering and of death. When in God's providence it is necessary for the prophet to suffer at the hands of his fellows, God's love will sustain him. When in the garden he said to his son, "This is the cup," his son not only took it and drank it, but the Father's love sustained him through each bleak and terrible moment of the ensuing ordeal.

The God he found in life was the Lord of life eternal. For to know this God, to love him, to serve him, is to break through the fleeting, the temporary, and the ephemeral and thus to know the meaning of that which truly endures forever because it is of God.

Jesus not only found God in life; he found himself in the service of God and became the one in whom men not only find God but find themselves. We never know ourselves more truly or deeply as we are until we know ourselves as we are known by God in Christ.

I beg of you, do not let these complicated theological

terms keep you from catching a very simple fact and taking it as food for your spirit: the love of God which we see in Jesus Christ and which he found in life is an all-sustaining, all-embracing, all-sufficient love. It will not let us go. God can be depended upon; his love can be depended upon in life or in death; he is the one in whom we live and move and have our being. To know him is to know the meaning of life eternal. One of the best-loved verses in our New Testament is this: "For God so loved the world that he gave his only Son, that whoever believes in him should not perish but have eternal life." The God whom Jesus Christ found in life is the one through whom eternal life has been made possible to every human being—even persons like us!

3. He Made Love
a Live Option

Scripture: *Luke 7:36-50*

Text: *She loved much.*

I

The word "option" has infiltrated the vocabulary of daily life. It means basically "choice." When a mother asks of her son, "What are you going to do?" she is inquiring into the options before him. When the chairman of the board of one of our great industries was making his annual report, he concluded with a section titled "The Options Before Us." Option, then, is a kind of open door through which action may proceed. It is an alternative, a choice that may or may not be chosen. As such, it is essential to responsible living, to freedom, to growth, and above all to faith.

Options are of two sorts: *dead* and *live*. A dead option is one that is no longer open, a choice which is no longer possible, an alternative we may no longer consider in a realistic way. The landscape of life is dotted with such.

I find it interesting to hear scholars discuss the once living but now dead options of history. At a recent meeting of one of their associations a number of historians were discussing with great learning and vigor: What if the West had not pulled Hitler off Russia in 1941? What if the United States had entered the League of Nations in 1920 with real determination and power? What if the United States, instead of intervening in South Vietnam unilaterally from 1954 on to our own time, had chosen to lay the entire matter where it properly belonged, then and now, namely, before the United Nations? While some of these options are not quite as dead as others, all of them indicate doors through which we may no longer walk as a result of choices now closed to us.

In personal life the same thing holds true. We can recall many options along the line of the years of our lives. And it is an interesting thing to realize that when we choose one option, that choice itself makes other options dead. This plainly is or ought to be the case in marriage. Until the decision to marry is made by two persons, each is confronted by a number of other options. But when the decision to marry is made, and they are actually married, all other options are closed—or ought to be. They are as dead as though they "had not been," to use Job's phrase.

The birth of a child opens certain possibilities for the parents and forever closes others. For the coming of a child into a family remakes the total situation for everyone involved. Not that there will be radical breaks with all other relationships and responsibilities, but there will be a profound recentering of the lives, the loyalties, the efforts, the plans, and the dreams of the parents by the opening of the door of life in and through their child.

We discover the operation of a live option in the choice we make for the profession we are going to follow. It takes many years to prepare for any major professional career now. And one needs to be quite sure in his own mind as to his interests, loyalties, and personal fitness for a profession before he ever starts on the long career of training. If one is interested in being a minister and starts on that course of preparation, it will ill serve him if he should later choose to be a dentist. While there are some painful similarities between the two professions, they are more a matter of practice than preparation!

There is always an element of nostalgia about dead options:

> For of all sad words of tongue or pen,
> The saddest are these: 'It might have been!'

Yet it is easy to weep too much over the might-have-beens of life. Life streams on and keeps confronting us with new and living options.

While we may no longer confront the option of whether or not we should have intervened in South

43

Vietnam unilaterally in 1954, there are a number of very live options confronting us as we face the conflict there now. One that many of us have been pleading for since 1954 has recently been chosen under radically different circumstances, namely, the presentation of the war in Vietnam to the United Nations with power granted to act. It is entirely possible that we are taking this step much too late for effective functioning on the part of that organization, but whether or not this is so, the step has finally been taken. There are other options in connection with the conflict: we do not need to escalate the war in Vietnam; we can heed the pleas of 90 percent of the people in the world, including all church groups, and cease the bombing of North and South Vietnam alike; we can throw our unqualified weight behind an all-Asian conference approach to a reappraisal of what ought to be done in Southeast Asia. Options like these are now before us. Whether we should be there is a dead option, but how to get out with credit and with some sense of responsibility for our having been there is a very live option.

It is important to keep our attention centered upon the live options that confront us both personally and collectively. Dead options are dead, and while they may be of importance to the historian and some of their lessons may be of importance to all of us, we must keep facing forward if we are going to live responsibly.

One of the very great dangers of growing old—personally and institutionally—is the blurring of the difference between dead and live options. While some of this may be relatively innocent, it can also be extremely dangerous.

I recall with a good deal of vividness one of the most interesting neighbors I had in boyhood. He was an aged Confederate soldier. He seemed to plod through each day with a minimum of excitement about anything, that is, until he began to talk about the great war and the Battle of Gettysburg, in which he fought. Then the old man would come alive and discuss what Longstreet did, what Lee and Pickett should have done! He was a different person—so different that we loved to get him going on the Civil War just to observe the difference! But when he had completed his involvement in what was easily the most exciting moment of his life, he would lapse back into the plodding life of a small rural town in the late twenties, where it made no earthly difference what Longstreet, Lee, or Pickett should have done so many years ago on the fateful battlefield of Gettysburg.

I have known people to live with dead options as though they were alive, and always it has led to disaster. I think of a young family who came to New York City a number of years ago. The move was made in order to broaden the father's professional training and to give him experience he could not secure elsewhere. It was a professional move entirely and a very good one, professionally. But he and his family could not accept the changed status of their life in the city. They seemed to regret the move to New York with increasing bitterness with each passing day. They kept harking back to the days when they were in Iowa, kept recalling what they had there but did not have here, kept reminding themselves of how much better off their children would have been had they stayed in Iowa rather than moving to New York City. All these considerations had real merit but they had one consequence that was completely disastrous for the parents: they unfitted them completely for the options that were open in New York City. They did not see what was here to be seen; they did not enter into the incredible richness, variety, and significance of the life of this city. They regarded it as a prison, rather than the most significant city on the face of this earth. Finally, their loyalty to the dead options both betrayed and defeated the legitimate hopes and dreams that had brought them to New York, and they returned to Iowa with a tremendous sense of bitterness over the entire experience. Difficult as it is to live in New York City, where there is upon occasion an equal mixture of grit and glamor, the simple fact is that a good many million people find it possible to live in this unparalleled concentration of business and cultural activity that can minister to the unfolding life of anyone who is open to it.

One of the many secrets of success in personal relationships, then, is to be able to distinguish between live and dead options and to choose the living, no matter how difficult it may be. I think so often of the very sensible yet agonizing statement of a wife who was trying to find the strength to keep her marriage alive in the face of her husband's admitted infidelity. He was confident that this one experience would be the last, and there was some reason to believe in his integrity in this matter, but the final decision lay with his wife. The option she once faced of a marriage of complete confidence in him unmarred by any transgression against it was dead. She had to face a new option, one on which the marriage itself depended. And she faced it with real glory, saying, "We must move ahead together—somehow. I am sure our love is still alive and may become strong enough to give us confidence in each other again."

I will not need to press the relevance of this distinction between dead and live options and the necessity of confronting the live ones to religious people. Certainly we face it in religion in general, in the Christian religion, in the Christian church, and in our own individual churches in very special ways, do we not?

There may have been a time when we could speak of a Christian Europe—as indeed there was in the Middle Ages—but no longer. There may have been a time when we could speak of America as a Christian country, meaning by this that by and large it was devoted to the Christian understanding and interpretation of life, but no longer. There may have been a time when we could take for granted the claim that man is a religious being, but even that is now coming under heavy dispute. Actually, we face an awesome list of questions wherever we turn in religion these days, but they boil down to one fundamental question: "Do the so-called fundamentals of faith have any relevance at all today?" Is faith in God a live or a dead option? Is faith in the kingdom of God a live or a dead option? Is faith in Jesus Christ a live or a dead option?

II

In this book we are testing the credibility of our faith in Jesus Christ by studying the things he did and trying to find out whether they open live options in our own understanding of the life we must live today. Obviously, we cannot go back to live with him in the first century A.D. in Palestine. It is a rich experience to walk the roadways over which he himself may have walked, but to do so today does not create any of the options he faced then. What we must ask is whether or not a deep encounter with him and his spirit as we find it in his deeds opens options that are really alive for us today, options we would not see if we did not look at life through his eyes and with his spirit, in so far as we are able to do this.

We need to look most carefully at the idea of love as we find it expressed in and through him and ask whether it is a live or a dead option. As far as the records go, he found in it a live option—one in which he acted—and he believed in it so deeply that he made it a live option for his followers. What did he see in love that made it all-important?

For him love is an act that men must choose to engage in. Love is always an act, a deed, a projection of self through choice into a human situation. His life and teachings make this abundantly clear.

In little children he saw what others did not see, namely open doors to the kingdom of God. He makes the negative point that it would be better for a man to be drowned than to injure one of them and the positive point that we must be willing to receive the kingdom of God in the spirit of a little child, if we are to receive it at all.

There was the time the multitudes had followed him and his disciples into a secluded place in the desert where they were having a quiet and probing conversation. His disciples were all for sending them away and letting them shift for themselves when it came mealtime, but this he refused to do. He had compassion on them and ministered to their needs, speaking to them and feeding them as best he could. People were never crowds to him. Multitudes were men and women; they were the children of God through whom God was trying to work a mighty work. He dedicated himself to the task of helping people find themselves and be true to the God who was trying to help them.

We see this especially in his dealing with sinners like the woman who broke into a feast given in his honor, seeking only to bathe his feet and dry them with her hair. The host wanted her thrown out as one who defiled their august and righteous company. Jesus would have none of this. He was moved with compassion toward her and said to the host, "She loves much," and because of her great love her sins are forgiven.

In Jesus' dealing with religious leaders he was deeply troubled by the fact that they let their loyalty to the Law bar their awareness of the new things the love of God was seeking to bring to pass. They were putting ritual before obedience. They had lost the spirit of the Law in obedience to the letter of the Law. He argued

49

with them, pleaded with them, defied them, did every-thing he could to awaken them to the enormity of the sin of not letting the openness of God's love become a living fact in their lives.

Love caused Jesus to identify himself with his enemies in an unusual way. He said it is both necessary and pos-sible to love your enemies. He never treated them as enemies; they were always human beings. He could always pray of them, "Father, forgive them; for they know not what they do."

Love caused him to deal with his disciples with a kind of patience and understanding that is hard to believe. They wanted to call down fire on villages that had mis-treated them, but he said, "No, that is not the way." When they wrangled over their status in the coming kingdom of God, he dealt with them firmly, yet com-passionately. And even after his death in his encounter with Peter he had everything turn on the question asked three times over, "Do you love me?" And when Peter replied that he did, Jesus said, "Feed my sheep."

For Jesus Christ, love was not only a live option; it was a dangerous one as well. It called for a radical reeval-uation of thought and life. It called for the reduction of thirteen hundred or more commandments, written out and treasured in sacred scroll, to two great command-ments: to love God and to love neighbor. No wonder the scribes thought him blasphemous—reducing the whole code of commandments of the fathers to two com-mandments, both of which revolve around love itself!

Love for him called for a radical reevaluation of

loyalty. Love was the prelude to what can only be called a most profound radicalism in life. He never tried to disguise the fact that his disciples were off on a radical venture if they followed him. The token of discipleship was clear: "By this all men will know that you are my disciples, if you have love for one another." The test of discipleship was whether they were willing to serve one another. The measure of greatness among his disciples was the number of people they served. His disciples must take up their crosses daily and follow him; they must face and endure persecution for his sake; they must follow him unto death; they must put loyalty to him above all other loyalties—to parent, temple, way of life.

Actually, the revolution implied in acceptance of the idea of love was best summed up in the apocryphal Gospel of Philip in this one verse which I wish had somehow or other found its way into our New Testament, "Unless you change your 'down' to 'up' and 'up' to 'down' and 'right' to 'left' and 'left' to 'right' you shall not enter my kingdom!"

The most eloquent and magnificent understatement in history is the biblical word, "Behold, I make all things new." The New Testament shouts "Amen" to this on every page. For the men who walked through those pages were not hashing over bygones, dreaming idle dreams, debating dead options. They were certain they had chosen a live option; they had entered an open door to a new life and were simply reporting that experience to others who had before them a similar opportunity. And while any summary of the rich experience of the New Testament days of course leaves much out, their reports reduce to those facts that had changed their lives. They said, "In Jesus Christ we have found and have been found by the love of God. We meet it full force and face to face. This can happen to you, and if it does, it will change your life." Ask them why this is so, and they can think of no other answer than the familiar verse, "For God so loved the world that he gave his only Son, that whoever believes in him should not perish but have eternal life." For they were convinced that in Jesus Christ, God had opened a new era for all men—one of love and hope.

The love of God which they proclaimed is a mercy that pardons and a joy that transforms. They insisted that what we do in love is an act of obedience, even as what we do without love is an act of disobedience to God. Love is our only appropriate response to his love for us. The priority and power of divine love are the most significant facts in the Christian experience.

Therefore the New Testament writers asked themselves what God expects of all who enter the open door of love. And their answer was quick and clear: obedience through a life of love manifest in service. This obedience lifted them out of a "natural" self and "normal" life into a new self and a new life. They would not have understood our desire to be normal persons. They wanted to be deeply abnormal persons, as the world views abnormality. They wanted to be creatures of and servants of the love of God, for this love is the fulfillment of and the only authentic seal of loyalty to the Christian faith.

III

Generations later when serious Christian thinkers were trying to put their faith into formal theological form in order to share it intelligently with generations far removed from New Testament days, times, and situations, they developed the doctrine of the Incarnation, which is a way of saying in precise theological language that "God was in Christ reconciling the world to himself, . . . and entrusting to us the message of reconciliation." This doctrine of the Incarnation is itself the first movement in a continuing effort to state clearly and forcefully the true meaning of the Christian faith. It is an attempt to explain how and why the love of God entered human life and history with such force and power in Jesus Christ. It seeks to explain to the church her true mission, nature, and meaning in the world. She is to be a servant, an obedient servant of the love of God which came to man in Jesus Christ. The doctrine is a forceful and unique one, claiming that the forgiving love of God has completely changed the human situation.

But the doctrine of the Incarnation itself is not simply a recapitulation of what happened in the past; it calls upon Christians who have received the forgiving love of God to share it with others. The deeds of love of a Christian are a part of the continuing deed of God's love in Jesus Christ. God by his act of love in Jesus Christ introduced a new order of being and reality in the world. That is the new option in the Christian faith. It is a live option; it is an option open to all men, and as one shares in it, he becomes the obedient instrument of the love of God.

Interestingly, as the various branches of Christendom are groping toward each other today in the ecumenical movement, we are finding that the one doctrine on which there is complete agreement is the doctrine of the Incarnation. This is as it should be since it continues to tell us who we are as a church; it answers our search for identity and indicates the direction of mission and service. It relates us to all other human beings in such fashion that life makes sense and human beings and human relations have ultimate meaning.

Students of Paul Tillich discover his profound regard for the truth of the doctrine of the Incarnation, even though he seldom deals with it directly. For the truth of it, to him, is the truth of the whole of our religious heritage. While Tillich confesses that the notion that God is love is a mystery for finite understanding, he insists that it is an essential symbol for conveying the proper meaning of God. He says, "The process of divine life has the character of love." And when pushed for amplification of this, he says, "God works toward the fulfillment of every creature and toward the bringing-together into the unity of his life all who are separated and disrupted."

The New Testament has our Lord saying to his disciples, "My Father is working still, and I am working," and the doctrine of the Incarnation of this love causes this very sentence to read, "We work and our Father works in us." It puts a full end to any effort to separate

God and Christ as some of our radical theologians are bidding us do. Any attempt to separate the love of God from the life of Jesus Christ reminds me of what a little girl said who had been terrified by Calvinist teachings about the cruelty of God, "I hate God but love Jesus." Wherever one feels this way, there has been some poor instruction in the nature of the love of God. For God and Jesus Christ are one in the fact of love, in the divine compassion which all men feel as they come into his presence.

I do not suppose twentieth century man has a greater need than to discover for himself that love continues to be a live option. Love is more a service than a sentiment though; it is more a relationship than an idea; it is more an actual, ethical, and moral projection of life, than a dream or a hope.

IV

What follows for us if we treat love as a live option? It is not an easy or a safe choice; it is an exacting and a dangerous one—as the world weighs danger. If our day is no longer impressed by the relevance of the church, then we have only ourselves and our disobedience to the Lord of love to blame. If the gospel we preach is greeted with a bored yawn rather than a marshalling of energy and life in its service, then we are not preaching the gospel of the love of God as a live option. Any Christian in his right mind would rather be greeted by a howling mob than by a congregation of bored yawns.

We belong in the depths of every human problem and controversy, for the love of God is there and seeks effective ministry and interpretation. We bring to each controversy not necessarily a more informed knowledge of details, but an ultimatum, a divine ultimatum which has to do with ultimate meanings and relationships. We say, "This do, and live." We say, "Let the humanness of human beings be exalted in this situation, for only then can the love of God be served." We must love greatly in order to be the servants of love. We must learn to look with the eyes of love, to become as little children; then we shall see God as God and men as the children of God and as human beings. To see them as such is to want to share deeply in the glory and the tragedy of human life.

Jesus Christ made love a live option. Made it? Yes, in the exact sense that he found it to be a live option. He found that it is possible to look at people with the eyes of love and find much in them that is deeply and truly lovable. He found that it is possible for one to speak and act in the spirit of love in any situation and to know the sustaining power of God through it all. He never walked alone; he always walked with God; he sought to know and to serve God in the spirit of love among all men. And he expects no less from his disciples.

Love for us outranges morals and moral conventions. It enables us to "hate the sin, yet love the sinner." It requires of us never to give up on any human being no matter who he is or what he has done. It requires of us, further, that we move directly into every situation where human beings are in conflict with each other and try to be the one through whom a compassionate mediating spirit of the love of God can find articulation and expression. That, as I understand it, is the contemporary interpretation of a very old verse: "By this all men will know that you are my disciples, if you have love for one another."

4. He Healed the Ill

Scripture: *Matthew 8:1-17; Luke 2:41-52*

I

Sickness and health are among the oldest and most puzzling facts of human life. Man has always felt their power and sought to avoid sickness by whatever means at hand. He has also been forced to try to understand them in the light of his experience. The record of his efforts to understand and cope with illness is the record of the growth of our understanding of our bodies, our minds and, indeed, of the science of medicine itself. This is a long record, disappearing in the mists of prehistory. It contains within its pages—inscribed sometimes on the walls of caves in southern France or deduced from fossils uncovered in Africa or incarnate in legends, spells, and incantations—a stirring tribute to man's determination to understand and if at all possible to cope with sickness and death, the great threats to life itself.

What could be more normal than that man's understanding of sickness in any given period is part and parcel of his knowledge and understanding of the world in which he lives? Early man's understanding of sickness was an integral part of his total understanding of the world. It is a far cry from our understanding of it in a medical center like New York City—though I am informed that even in this city there are some appallingly primitive understandings and prescribed cures for illnesses. We do live on the face of the same planet, but we do not live in the same world as primitive man.

Early man believed the world to be the abode not alone of men, but of good and evil spirits. Such spirits were, to adapt Tennyson's word: "Closer . . . than breathing, and nearer than hands and feet." They vied with each other over man and his welfare. The evil spirit would deceive, hurt, and misguide him if possible while the good spirit would try to ward off the ravages of the evil spirit and help man in every other way. Sickness was regarded as the work of an evil spirit that somehow had sneaked into man's life and was distorting it.

This control of man by spirits fitted in with early man's understanding of himself. Phrased differently in different cultures and ages, the general idea of early man was that he had a body, a mind, and a spirit, with the spirit actually controlling mind and body. His spirit was a true member of the spirit world. And when man slept, his spirit might leave his body and roam abroad. How else could he explain the helplessness of the body in

59

sleep or the fact that in dreams a man can actually encounter other people? His spirit would invade the vacated body of another in dreams and would actually control and disturb the sleeper—thus early man regarded dreams.

Illness was regarded in prescientific cultures as the result of an evil spirit invading the life of a person. It would come as punishment for sin. The evil spirit might either be sent by God or by a spell or a charm from some enemy. We have many recorded cases among primitive peoples that continue to exist in certain parts of the world of individuals sickening and actually dying because they believed that an evil spirit had taken possession of them.

Bronislaw Malinowski, an anthropologist who specialized in the South Sea Island cultures, tells of the minute care with which some tribes search every tree and other possible hiding place for objects that might house evil spirits placed there by their enemies. The Pueblo Indians in the southwestern part of the United States have many lively beliefs about evil spirits and how to deal with them. And so it goes in the early age of man wherever we find him. Henry Sigerist of Johns Hopkins University begins his monumental book *On the History of Medicine* not in the laboratories of the great hospitals, but in the abodes of demons, evil spirits, charms, spells, and weird incantations in odd and out-of-the-way temples and holy places of primitive man. But medicine was not alone in this company; all our sciences were there in exceedingly primitive form.

II

The struggle toward a rational understanding of life and sickness has been a long one; even now it is far from a finished journey. So we shall not wonder overmuch to discover that the Old and New Testaments reflect the understanding of sickness that was prevalent in the ages in which they were written. Who seriously could expect it to have been otherwise?

To be sure, we have glints of a reasoned approach to some kinds of illness and disease in scripture, and out of these medicine as we know it today begins to emerge. But this is the exception and not the rule. The rule can be stated quite simply: sickness is caused by an evil spirit that has managed to replace or subjugate the normal spirit of a human being. The cure of illness is just as obvious: chase the evil spirit out—exorcise it. We find in the Old Testament many carefully detailed rites for exorcising such demons. Sin itself was regarded as a kind of demon possession.

For the Hebrew, then, there were three causes of disease:

1. God was punishing the individual for his sin and had done so by sending an evil spirit to take possession of the person.

2. The ill person was suffering for the sins of his parents; the demon who caused the sickness was simply a tool in God's hand.

3. The ill person had been seduced by Satan—as was Job.

In every case the priest was the one to go to for the cure. And the priest had a cure in the form of a rite that was supposed to lure or scare the devil out of the ill person and actually overpower it by the superior power of a good spirit. The hospital for the early Hebrews was the temple; the operating room was the high altar; the chief doctor was the high priest; the therapeutical procedure was participation in the rites of exorcism and cleansing. Only then could a restoration of health be hoped for.

The understanding of illness was somewhat more advanced among the Greeks. But even in that remarkable culture there was a profound intermingling of religion and medicine. Twin deities presided over the health of men: Asclepias, the god of health, and Hygeia, the goddess of health. Both patient and doctor brought offerings to these deities when illness was to be treated. And the tradition of modern medicine continues to use the Hippocratic Oath, which took its early form in ancient Greece.

Even so, educated, sophisticated Greeks regarded illness as a disturbance in the mysterious elements that make up man. In health these elements were in symmetrical, harmonious pattern and proportion; in illness they were in disarray and disunity. The function of the doctor or priest was to restore inner harmony. Plato argued that education and a well-ordered life will achieve, maintain, and restore health. And, let it be noted, he had a very low opinion of doctors and their treatment of "burning, cutting, drugging and starving." Marcus

Aurelius—sometimes called the most civilized man produced in Rome—regarded illness as a punishment of the gods and bade the afflicted seek temples for healing.

III

It was in an environment shaped by these ideas that Jesus lived and the Christian church took form. Is it not, therefore, asking the impossible to seek modern ideas of medicine in the New Testament? Would it not be utterly irrational to think that Jesus or his disciples or Paul or other early Christian leaders should do other than share commonly held conceptions of health, sickness, and proper medical procedures?

The New Testament presents the early church, beginning with our Lord himself, as children of the age and culture in which they lived and of which they were an integral part. For the early church there was no gap between religion and medicine; they were inseparably interwoven ways of healing ill human beings. This we must always bear in mind as we study the deeds of Christ in curing the sick.

If we would understand and appreciate the relationship between what we separate into the different categories of religion and medicine as these are found in the New Testament, we must proceed with care. Several stepping stones will usher us into a workable understanding of it:

1. The age-old fear of illness and desire for good

health are present in every person pictured in the New Testament.

2. The desire for cures is as omnipresent as the fact of illness, and healing is sought at the shrines of village and city alike.

3. Illness, from the beginning of our records, has been regarded as evidence of divine displeasure, with the afflicted person always asking, "Why is God doing this to me?"

4. One of the works of the eagerly-awaited Messiah of the Hebrews will be to heal the sick, the lame, the broken-hearted, and raise the dead.

5. Healing is understood as a sign of forgiveness and a restoration of God's favor.

6. Healers were to be found on every hand; every forceful religious leader from Moses to Jesus of Nazareth is reported to have performed many miracles including the miracle of healing, if not actually raising from the dead. Understandably, then, Christ is presented in the New Testament as the healer of those who are ill.

7. But Christ is not alone in being presented this way; his disciples and later the apostles were credited with miraculous cures over illness.

8. In every case illness and demon possession were thought to be identical. Once the demon was exorcised or removed, health and normalcy would be restored.

According to the Gospel records our Lord healed in four different ways: through prayer (Mark 9:29), by the use of an ointment of clay and saliva (John 9:6), by the influence of his presence (Luke 8:43-44), and by the touch of his hands (Mark 5:41). The disciples and apostles were credited with cures wrought by the laying on of hands (Mark 16:18) and prayers uttered "in the name of Jesus" (Acts 3:6).

All sorts of healing miracles can be found in the pages of the Four Gospels. Three times the dead are raised, several times leprosy is healed, hemorrhages are stopped, sight is restored to the blind, the lame walk, persons barred from normal communities as lunatics are restored to normal life, behavior, and association. And so it goes. Was it not pathetic, wistful, wonderfully prophetic, the way in which the people of Palestine brought their ill to him for curing? He was the one to whom they turned in their deepest needs. Believing as they did that healing came when they were reestablished in God's favor and the evil spirits driven from within them, to whom else should they turn than to one hailed as the Messiah, the special messenger of God, one empowered by God to bring the spirit of healing to all persons of faith?

IV

So much for the records. Now to the hard question that must be asked clearly even if we are not able to answer it to the satisfaction of all: Did these things really happen?

Who can say? The Gospel records affirm them, but they are not peculiar to the Gospels. Similar miracles are affirmed in the literature of Greeks and Romans alike. We do not understand how many of these miracles of healing could have happened because we no longer see them or anything like them occurring around us now. I know the fact that we do not see them now is not conclusive evidence that they did not happen then. But the circumstantial evidence of what we know now makes it highly unlikely that they did happen then or any other time. We are not obligated, in the name of honest piety, to affirm or accept as true all claims made in the name of piety in earlier ages. The dead may have been raised then—we have only the records to go on—but the dead are no longer being raised; about this there is no doubt at all.

The healing miracles are of widely different sorts— some credible, others frankly not. Modern medicine affirms the inseparability of emotion and physiology. In some ailments disordered emotions are the prime factor in illness; a distorted emotion is as concrete an ailment as a broken leg. In others the courage to face illness realistically, the will to live, is a prime factor in recovery. In others simple anxiety long sustained can actually lead to various kinds of physiological disorders with headaches, stomach disorders, tics, and various kinds of skin ailments. We have learned much about the relationship between emotional shocks and mental and physiological disorders.

During World War II, I served as religious counselor for conscientious objectors in Maryland. I had referred to me upon one occasion a young man, an expert rifleman in actual training, who had suddenly developed an incapacity to pull the trigger of his rifle. His finger simply froze. After a while we stumbled onto the fact that his Quaker mother had drummed into him from earliest infancy, "Thou shalt not kill," and now a literal fixation had suddenly developed as he was being readied for actual combat. Fortunately for all, he was transferred to the medical corps, where he served out the remainder of the war.

This leads to the obvious point that many, but not all, of the healing miracles are credible in the light of our own experience today. So when someone asks me whether I believe in the miracles of the New Testament, that is, whether I believe them possible, I must ask, "Which ones?" Some I can credit; others I cannot, and I see no honest way to avoid this distinction. Some may say, "Well, I must believe all or none; therefore I believe them all," and I shall not dispute their right to say it, but neither will I stake my faith on that kind of supposition. For my faith must stand on what I can believe to be true, on what in my experience I understand to be reasonable and possible. I refuse to hang it upon the nail of impossible miracles predicated upon records of other ages.

To me, healing is as wonderful a mystery when brought about in our hospitals as in our temples of faith. The war on sickness is as urgent and desperate when we are after viruses and germs as when we were after devils. Health as a condition of well-being is as true an ideal for men when sought through medicine as through the ministrations of faith itself.

But I must confess to being a conservative, perhaps a

reactionary, in one regard: I refuse to separate medicine and religion; I cannot because they both deal with human beings. I am forced by hard-won experience, however, into a different understanding of the proper relationship between religion and medicine than that which was obtained in earlier ages.

Nor am I, a religionist, alone in this. Nearly every medical center in the United States not only would understand it, but has moved to implement it. There is now a close cooperation between religion and medicine, and we shall see it come even closer over the years and generations ahead. We recognize the interrelations that exist between our two disciplines, and we are seeking a better understanding of what this interrelationship means and how we can strengthen each other by it. The chaplain's service at our hospitals is a token of this mutual need. And we must never forget that the age-old determination of the church to build, maintain, and support hospitals is a similar token of the high regard which religion has for medicine. There is no longer any reason why the priest should try to play the doctor or the doctor the priest. Both are essential to the effective treatment of major ailments which threaten the life and well-being of a human being. It is unmitigated tragedy for doctor and minister alike when they are set against each other. Both they and the ill person suffer needlessly when this occurs.

Yet it is not always easy to keep a sense of cooperation in this matter. I recall Dr. John Finney of Johns Hopkins University returning from a tour of the clinics sponsored by the mission stations in China in the early thirties. He said of them, "They are dispensing good gospel but poor medicine!" And this serves as warning that good medicine and rational religion can and must work together if both are to be truly helpful to human beings in pursuit of health.

V

As I have read and reread the Gospel narratives that set forth the life of our Lord, I am impressed by the fact that of the many ill people who came to him, some were cured and some were not. It depended really upon the nature of the illness that brought them there. Some of them did not even know they were ill; they were the ones he was hard put to cure. The ones he could not heal were the ones who refused to admit that they were ill.

He could not cure Pilate of his skepticism—and a mental disease will distort life as truly as a virus or a germ can ever distort a body.

He could not cure the crowds of their blindness to what he was trying to do, of their deafness to what he was trying to say. Finally, he was done to death by them —the very ones he had tried to cure.

He could not save Judas from the bitter despair that swept over him when Jesus did not prove to be the kind of Messiah he wanted. The thirty pieces of silver represent an honest valuation of what Judas thought of himself as well as what he thought of the messianic claims of Jesus Christ.

He could not cure the religious leaders of his people of their self-righteousness, of their blind adherence to rite, form, and tradition, of their unwillingness to have their eyes opened to the new things God was trying to bring to pass round about them.

But Jesus could and did and will continue to cure people who come to him in search of a relationship with God that will bring to the full the capacities they have. He did cure Mary Magdalene of her life of sin and set her on the road toward a new life. He did cure many of the sense of despair and helplessness men inevitably feel when they are separated from God. As one of the healed ones said, "You have the words of eternal life." And millions in subsequent ages have stood up to make the same affirmation, that in and through him they have found a fullness of life, an abundant life because of what he brought.

The struggle for sanity in what appears to be an insane world has never been and will never be an easy one. The most grievous ailments of our time are spiritual, not physiological. Cancer, I know, is a great killer, but hatred is a greater one. The hatred and blindness that erupt in and support war will kill more men in the prime of life, will cripple and kill more women and children, will cause more authentic deformities, today and in succeeding generations, than any other ailment known to men.

One young surgeon coming back from the hospitals of World War II said to me in anguish, "Why don't you fellows settle down to the job of stopping this business of killing? All we surgeons can do is patch up the pathetic pieces that remain after men have been blown apart." And as he spoke, I realized all over again the need for Jesus Christ, the one who can cure the most desperate illnesses of our time. For in him we discover the fact of love, the power of love, and the need for love if our lives are to be whole, if our relationships are to be creative and helpful, if our world is ever to emerge from the jungle of prejudice, war, malice, and hate to walk on the high plateaus of goodwill and brotherhood.

But for this to happen we must be conscious of our illness; we must come to him in search of healing. We need Jesus Christ, the healer of men; we need the ministry of his love; we can be made whole again only as we subject ourselves to the therapy of that love and are willing to become the children of it each day that we live.

It it with good cause, then, that we hail him as the great physician and seek to identify ourselves with every movement in the human enterprise that seeks to cure man from the illnesses from which he suffers, whether physiological, mental, or spiritual. For we are an ill people, and we need the ministry of divine love if ever we are to find our way toward wholeness, the kind of wholeness God intended in creation. In a very real sense, then, speaking quite literally, we say of Jesus Christ he is the healer of men. In and through him we find the meaning of true health and true wholeness.

5. He Judged Men

Scripture: *Matthew 7:1-14*

I

There is not much point in talking about Jesus as a judge unless we can do something about the usual connotations of the notion of a judge. The very word conjures up a veritable cluster of ideas—some of which fit Jesus and some of which do not.

"Judge," as we see the term in ordinary life, indicates one who represents the civil government in hearing and settling disputes by rendering a verdict himself or by taking the verdict of a jury and announcing or determining the nature of the judgment. But, in any event, when the judge speaks officially, a dispute is settled (unless right of appeal or reconsideration are available and used). As Adam Clayton Powell discovered, not even a congressman can forever avoid abiding by a duly authorized verdict of a judge.

The Advisory Committee on Peace of the National

Council of Churches met with Ambassador Goldberg shortly after he had left the Supreme Court for his post in the United Nations. In the course of his comments on this change, he said that the thing he missed most was the right to write what he called the four greatest words he knew, the ones with which the decisions of the Supreme Court end: "It is so ordered."

Jesus, as we shall see, could, would, and did pass judgments on men, but they were not of this kind. They were the judgments of a teacher, a prophet, a friend, not those of one appointed to hear disputes, to administer the law, and to determine judgment.

When we think of a judge, we think of one whose business it is to adjudicate actual disputes between and among men. For without men in serious dispute, we would have little or no need for judges.

While Jesus did upon occasion deal with men in sharp dispute, as a rule he did not. Even when he did, the disputes were not of a kind to take to a court of law. The younger brother in the parable of the prodigal son had a legal right to make a fool of himself, and the elder brother had a legal right to make an even bigger fool of himself, yet Jesus did what no regular judge would have done: he judged between them. Who will say that his judgment did not deal with issues vital to both brothers (and to us) even though both acted well within the law of the land?

We think of a judge as one who is a servant to the spirit and word of the written law of a people. It is his high duty to observe the law and see that other men do likewise.

The people among whom Jesus lived had two kinds of law, courts, and judges: religious and civil. Rome granted Jewish authorities great freedom in the field of religious law, permitting them to administer and enforce it unless it should run beyond or counter to civil law. The temple authorities, for example, were permitted armed men in sufficient numbers to keep the peace in the temple, and possibly in other areas on holy days. Naturally, Rome kept a firm grip on all civil law and asserted its priority when it clashed with religious law. The Jews had their courts for hearing cases dealing with religious law; the Roman governor of a province had his courts for civil law, retaining, as Rome expected him to do, final responsibility in every case, religious and civil alike.

Jesus repeatedly went beyond and violated the letter of accepted religious law—and upon occasion the spirit of it too. This explains why the Pharisees and the lawyers skilled in Jewish law were set against him. And that is why Pilate finally, almost casually, gave in to the demands of the Jewish leaders for his death. They charged him with violating their law—a charge that had some truth in it—and threw in the charge of sedition, which they knew would bring Pilate's full attention to bear on the case.

So we shall not think of Jesus as a judge as we use the term in ordinary discourse, or even as they used it then. Why, then, you ask, do we say he judged men?

In answer let us get some general notions of the scope of his judgments, then examine some of them more closely before asking whether we as nominal disciples are called upon to judge men as he did.

II

He knew in his own experience the meaning of judgment. How could anyone live for thirty years without being molded by the multiple forms in which it enfolded his and all life? No one would have to urge the value of sound judgments on one brought up in the carpenter's trade. For in that work he judged materials and men all the time. He had to judge between materials to be used: wood or stone, which kind of stone; he had to judge the worth of what the customer wanted. I wonder whether Jesus was ever called to a home and asked to build a table or chest for the lady of the house and then told exactly how he should do it. I'm sure that must have happened! Maturing as he did in a province addicted to revolution, he learned to judge the worth of fanatical ideas. He had to learn it lest he be swept into one of the several abortive assaults on Rome which originated in Galilee. With a great caravan route of the Golden Crescent running past his door, he was exposed to at least the fragments of the religions and cultures of the ancient world. He had to weigh them against his own—and his own against them.

Life has a way of forcing judgments upon us and making judges of sorts of us all. Good judgment is not necessarily a matter of a formal education in the law, civil or religious. Some of the wisest and fairest men I've known in my life never got beyond grade school. But they learned how to size up a person or a situation; they judged people fairly. This was impressed on my mind by an older man in one of my first churches. Soon after going to the church I was asked to recommend the local school-teacher, whom I had not yet met, for a better job in a nearby town. On the next Sunday afternoon at the gathering of a huge family clan, I asked about the teacher. I was literally deluged with so many criticisms of her that I wondered whether she was fit to live, let alone teach. As I left, this old man, who had slipped out ahead of me, was waiting at the gate. He said, "Preacher, you can recommend her for that job. She's a fine young lady, good with the children and a good teacher." I must have looked my amazement because he added, "But she does aggravate the ladies a little."

Socrates put it nicely: "He who takes only a few things into account finds it easy to pronounce judgment." We see Jesus sizing up people and situations fairly and pronouncing judgments slowly but firmly.

Before proceeding further into the nature of his judgments we should take account of his admonition in the Sermon on the Mount to "judge not, that you be not judged." On the face of it this seems to deny us the right to judge anyone for any reason, but only on the face of it. Jesus is warning his disciples against the judgmental attitude which made religious leaders such a burden to him and to them. Some of these pious worthies were always telling people what was wrong and what was right with them. They so easily assumed that they had the right to pass such judgments. They were so busy hunting up the sins of others they had no time to be conscious of sins of their own. It was of such that Carlyle wrote: "The deadliest sin were the consciousness of no sin."

Jesus did not himself, nor did he want his disciples to, fall into this aggravating and obnoxious kind of judgment. He actually laughed at it by asking, "Why do you see the speck that is in your brother's eye, but do not notice the log that is in your own eye?" Or, as a theological student in New York City paraphrased it, "How can we see the speck in our brother's eye with so much smog in our own?"

Keeping this warning against superficial judgments in mind, Jesus nonetheless spent his public ministry judging men on the broadest possible front.

III

We get some notion of the scope of his judgments by a simple recital of fact:

He judged the ideas of men.

He judged the convention and institutions of men.

He judged the motives of men.

He judged the deeds of men.

And his judgments were directed at men on all levels of life, from an unnamed beggar to the high priest and the procurator, Pontius Pilate himself. It is safe to make some such generalization as this: whenever anyone or anything seemed to him to delay, deform, or deny the coming of the kingdom of God, he leveled a sharp judgment against it; whenever anyone or anything seemed to open the doors to the coming of that kingdom, he passed the judgment of praise upon it.

Just as our civil judges use the law as written and interpreted as a norm for judging a case, Jesus used the kingdom of God as his norm, or standard, for passing both negative and positive judgments. How could it have been otherwise? It was the call of God to preach the kingdom of God and to call men to citizenship in it that pulled him out of the carpenter's shop and propelled him into the public ministry. Once he emerged from the wilderness, one thing only dominated his every thought and action: the kingdom of God. This was the norm of his life; it determined all he said and did.

Without some such norm clearly in mind and dominating his own life, he would have continued as an unknown carpenter in the obscure town of Nazareth in the province of Galilee. But his devotion to the kingdom of God gave him a standard for determining what was good and what evil, what was worthy of loyalty and praise and what was not.

The most astounding thing about his judgments is the clarity and firmness with which they deal with sacred institutions like the temple, synagogue, and sabbath; with the accepted religious leaders: the scribes, pharisees, Sadducees, and priests; and with hallowed expectations and hopes like those centering in the Messiah. Criticizing any one of these would ensure trouble, but to weigh them all in the balances and proclaim them wanting guaranteed disaster. Small wonder that almost from the first day of his public ministry such tactics alienated some, angered others, and proved to be a festering wound in his relationship with his contemporaries.

The sabbath was the most widely observed and the most hallowed religious institution of Jesus' contemporaries in Palestine. He had been brought up under the discipline of its many laws and observances. The "why" of it all must have pressed for answer deeper than tradition long before the kingdom of God became the one blazing reality in his life. But once that great conviction came, he had a new and full answer to the meaning of the sabbath. Important? Yes. All-important? No! What was more important? Proclaiming the kingdom of God and meeting the needs of men in the spirit of that kingdom! Of course his answer made no sense at all to those in whose mind sabbath observance was the ultimate norm of conduct and piety. But with the kingdom of God as the norm the sabbath was forced into a subordinate role.

Some of his contemporaries set great store by fasting as a manifestation of piety; some seem to have made a public show of themselves during the fast. Jesus placed no great stock in fasting itself, and none at all in a public parade of piety over it. If you fast, he advised, do so with such joy that no one even suspects what you are doing.

He gave the same advice to those who exhibited their

faith by long prayers at street corners "that they may be seen by men." He told them to go home, seek their most secluded room, shut the door, and pray to God to be heard by him and by no one else.

He challenged the comfortable and commonly held assumption that a wide gap separated the admitted saints from confessing sinners. He said that he could find no great difference on this score. Some people were crippled by sins of passion, others by sins of greed, and others by sins of pride. As far as he could see, one was as badly crippled as the other. Take Zacchaeus, for example. He was a very crooked and admittedly sinful money changer; his neighbors in turn were crippled by the sin of self-righteousness. Jesus reached out to both, but only Zacchaeus responded, so the record reads.

Our Lord judged the motives of men; in fact, for him that is where all judgment begins. In doing this and lifting it up to his disciples, he broke really new ground in the history of ethics. He denied that he was breaking the sacred Law, which dealt with deeds like murder, adultery, etc., and insisted that he was merely extending its spirit to cover the motives that led to such deeds. It was this bold enlargement of the Law that gave Christian ethics its most distinctive and penetrating thrust. Righteousness was no longer an affair of keeping an ethical ledger or coming out right on the moral computer. It came to be a matter of intention, will, and heart. He believed it necessary to "keep your heart with all vigilance; for from it flow the springs of life" (Proverbs 4:23). Note well this shift in emphasis from law to heart; it not only cost him his life, but it guarantees new life to all who honestly believe it to be true.

Lest we think it a matter of words, recall how seriously he took it to be true. I am thinking particularly of that unbelievable moment on the cross when he took note of one of his fellow sufferers who spoke kindly of him, then begged, "Jesus, remember me when you come in your kingly power." Jesus did not try to feed the details of this poor wretch's life into an ethical computer to see how he would fare. In a flash he saw the genuine and complete openness of this man's soul to God, an openness which swept everything he had ever done into the background. Jesus said, "Truly, I say to you, today you will be with me in Paradise." What a judgment that was! In that word he judged not only that man, but also the ones who had put him there, and the ones who were standing around the cross saying that the dying men were getting just what was coming to them. But the judgment does not stop there. By and through it he opened the gate to the very seat of God's unfathomable love for all men. From that time on, even until this very moment, Christians have talked about love rather than justice when thinking about God. A friend of mine, a wise old minister, put it well when told by a friend, "God will deal justly with us when we get over there." My friend looked at him for a moment, then said, "What I want is not justice but mercy." And so do we all, if we will be honest about it.

81

IV

If time permitted, we could add to this list of the ways in which he judged men: the money changers in the temple, the disciples who lacked faith, the multitude whose scale of values was upside down. But there are two things about his method of judging that deserve special attention.

He passed no blanket judgment on men, not even the scribes and Pharisees. He took each person and each situation on its own merits, dug beneath the surface of appearances to the human being himself, and spoke of God's will for him. Saint and sinner alike felt the probe of his spirit as he went to the level of deepest need and laid it bare.

But the most wonderful thing about his method of judging is this: he did not so much judge men as he caused them to judge themselves. He helped men see themselves for what they were; he opened to them the poverty of their lives, the gravity of their need for God, but he let them see it and say what they were going to do about it. To come close to him was and is to be led into the area of self-judgment.

This comes out vividly at the Last Supper. Speaking as much to himself as to them, he says that one of them is going to crack under the strain and betray him. Instead of interrogating each other they, to a man, interrogated themselves: "Lord, is it I?" And the question itself was in the form of a confession that each one had been wondering whether he had what it might take to keep faith on the morrow. Jesus did not try to answer the question for them; he let each man look for his own answer. Finally, Judas could stand it no longer. He left, went to the camp of the enemy, gave them directions as to how to find Jesus, offered to lead them there himself, and thus etched an inerasable judgment on himself for all to see.

Later in the courtyard of Pilate's palace, Peter went through the same terrible agony of self-judgment in the presence of his betrayal of loyalty, but he was able to recover both his faith and his loyalty.

The Golden Rule sums it up: "Whatever you wish that men would do to you, do so to them." There's nothing easy or superficial about that rule; it goes to the heart of an authentic Christian judgment of another. First we must judge ourselves, then move to the other, but do it all as before the God of both of us.

V

It's frightening to realize where all of this takes us today, isn't it? We are under the judgment of God, and we know it. We have been called to be among those who seek to be the ones through whom his judgments can be focused upon the swiftly moving events of our time. No amount of rationalization can relieve us of this duty before God.

Barbara Ward, one of the great Christian spirits of our time, has helped us phrase one of the most comprehensive judgments we must insist upon today. Writing in her book *Spaceship Earth*, she says:

One of the fundamental moral insights of the Western culture which has now swept over the whole globe is that, against all historical evidence, mankind is not a group of warring tribes, but a single, equal and fraternal community. Hitherto, distances have held men apart. Scarcity has driven them to competition and enmity. It has required great vision, great holiness, great wisdom to keep alive and vivid the sense of the unity of man. It is precisely the saints, the poets, the philosophers, and the great men of science who have borne witness to the underlying unity which daily life has denied. But now the distances are abolished. It is at least possible that our new technological resources, properly deployed, will conquer ancient shortage. Can we not at such a time realize the moral unity of our human experience and make it the basis of a patriotism for the world itself? [1]

We in this country have the duty and responsibility of pressing such judgments home even in days of war, but we must do it in love; we must measure our country as Jesus measured his people—against the standard of the kingdom of God. When we do this, someone is sure to say that the United States is no worse than any other country and a lot better than many. That I am sure is true, and I would take it for granted, but can we stop there? Must we not press the point that while our country must play a great role in this emerging world, she must do so without trying to dictate its nature? I

[1] New York: Columbia University Press, 1966.

confess that I am appalled by the increasing number of times when on important matters we pay little or no attention to the judgments of others, even our close friends. As one seasoned British observer put it some time back: "Is it that the United States can't hear what her friends say, or just won't listen to them?" I suspect he and many others think of what one preschooler said to another: "Okay, you can come along if you cooperate, and that means you have to do what I say."

What sort of judgment ought to be passed on the war in Vietnam? Shall we look for it in the policy statements of the White House or State Department? I doubt it. These statements will be filed in the archives and remembered only when dug up by research students looking for materials for dissertations in political science and diplomacy. I saw on TV what I take to be the record of the real judgment history is passing on us. It was the specter of six thousand innocent villagers pulled out of their ancestral homes in what our military men call the Iron Triangle, loaded into our trucks like cattle, and herded into refugee camps around Saigon, a city the villager in Vietnam hates with a holy hatred. Then we went to work with our magnesium and other fire bombs and leveled their villages, homes, orchards, and fields to the ground; we sent in our bulldozers to destroy the most sacred place for most Vietnamese families, their ancestral burial grounds. Let us not for one single moment think that any word spoken by President Johnson, Secretary Rusk, or General Westmoreland will last beyond the moment in which it is uttered, but that event in Vietnam will etch a picture of what we are on the mind and conscience of all Asia more deeply than all our fine words about democracy, freedom, and self-determination. As I saw those people being driven and dragged from their homes and heard the women crying as their homes receded, never to be seen again, I felt again the awful fact of judgment come hammering out of that TV set, and I begged God that in his mercy my grandchildren might not have to make bloody atonement for the sins of my generation. Yet if they do, they will not be the first to do so, though they will surely be the last.

As I finished writing this, the early morning sun broke through the clouds and fell on a print of Dali's "Crucifixion," which faces my desk in the study. And I saw it, as it were, for the first time. The cross high above the world yet with men looking up to it as their only hope, the only light in the picture centered on the cross and the one who is looking at it. Yet far off in the distance the black horizon is broken by a point of light which carries the promise of a new dawn and a new day.

That, I said to myself and now say to you, is the truth of it. The cross of Jesus Christ is the true judgment of this world, of his church, and of each one of us who name his name. The only light we have or can find comes from him. Only as we look to him and keep faith with what we see in him can we know the meaning of light, hope, faith. And it is this experience that provides the only hope we have for tomorrow. Even as he judged men in the light of the kingdom of God, so must we, and in his name.

6. He Preached the Gospel of the Kingdom of God

Scripture: *Matthew 13:31-50*

I

Not many will question the need for purpose in life. But some will wonder whether there is any necessary connection between a fundamental purpose and faith in God, as great religion claims, or what we can learn of purpose from Jesus Christ, as the Christian faith claims.

There are several ways of describing the importance of this. One such is contained in a description of a new film, *Blow-Up*. In an interview with the *Life* correspondent in Paris, Michelangelo Antonioni, famed Italian movie producer, says of this film:

87

The young people among whom my film is situated are all aimless, without any other drive but to reach that aimless freedom. Freedom that for them means marijuana, sexual perversion, anything. . . . What you get at the end doesn't interest me. . . . It's that conquest of freedom that matters. The pursuit of freedom gives man his most exciting moments. Once it's conquered, once all discipline is discarded, then it's decadence. Decadence without any visible future.[1]

Like these young people many of us find our lives shredded by many different purposes that seem to be of equal importance but have no overarching purpose that brings them all together into a meaningful pattern. Others of us in moments of honesty will confess that we have no great or significant purpose at all—large or small —in our lives, save taking care of number one. Still another way to describe the importance of purpose in life is to say that if democracy is defeated by communism in the current struggle for men's minds and policies, it will be because the men who believe in communism believe in it more deeply, passionately, and intelligently than we believe in democracy. The struggle of purpose with purpose is the first and decisive stage in the struggle for influence and power in human life and society.

If Christianity is overwhelmed by atheism in any or all of its many forms, it will be because we who profess to believe in Christianity actually refuse to accept as binding upon us the purpose of the Christian faith. That

[1] *Life*, January 27, 1967, p. 66.

is why it is so essential that we grasp both the meaning of purpose in life and the power of the Christian purpose as we find it in Christ and in his expectation of his disciples.

While the struggle for a meaningful purpose is a problem for young and old alike, it is the critical problem for young people between the ages of fifteen and twenty. I do not suppose there is any other five-year period in life when so many gloriously critical problems crowd in upon us and demand solution. We must choose our vocation, our companion for life, our philosophy of life, with parents, preachers, teachers, and older relatives all mixing in—and not always helpfully! The psychologist who tagged this five-year period as the "storm and stress" period of life knew what he was talking about.

I am sure young people will forgive me when I say it is wonderful to be young—once! But once is enough, really it is. Our heart is just not strong enough to stand it twice; we can hardly stand it once! That, I am convinced, is why God hurries us through the rapids of youth where life is exciting, daring, decisive, dangerous, and lets us pant for a while before starting to row over the long and relatively quiet stretch of middle age. Then, just when we begin to get comfortable, comes a decisive command to stand on the bank while our children shoot the rapids. I do believe it is easier to be in the boat trying to do it ourselves, than to be marooned on the bank while the ones we love are battling their way along. But what God ordains mortal man must accept, and none may make this trip for another.

II

It is appropriate that the scriptural background for our consideration of the relationship between religious faith and personal purpose should center in the one who is the center of our thought in the Christian tradition, Jesus of Nazareth. During his public ministry he had as rough a time of it as any person could. Yet actually the outline of the story of that ministry, while well known to most, will be missed by anyone who does not feel in it the triumphant power of a great purpose. For Jesus Christ had one great purpose: to preach the gospel of the kingdom of God. He opens his ministry with the stirring word, "Repent, for the kingdom of heaven is at hand." In parable after parable, in discussion after discussion, he drives home the point that men are actually entering into a new era in human history, one in which the kingdom of God becomes a living reality. But, you ask, and quite properly, what did he mean by the kingdom of God?

Jesus was sounding an old theme when he spoke of the kingdom of God—but in an utterly new way. In the Old Testament the kingdom of God indicated the tremendous fact that God is King and called attention to the majesty and the sovereignty of the Most High. Its meaning soon included the faith that the day would come when the rule of God would be effectively realized on earth as well as in heaven. After the experience of the Exile the Hebrew people regarded the advent of

90

the rule of God as something that would be brought in by One set apart by God, the Anointed One, the Messiah. This expectation was an essential part of the age-old hope of Israel, and Jesus had learned of it at Mary's knee and in the synagogue in Nazareth.

But when he began to preach the kingdom of God, he did so with a difference. He insisted that the kingdom was at hand, that men should prepare themselves for life in it. To be sure, it was the rule of God, but it was to manifest itself in love, compassion, understanding, and in the achievement of a society where men would love, trust, and work with one another as children of God.

As nearly as we can determine from a study of the New Testament records, the kingdom of God, for Jesus, was an event, not an idea. It was an actual gift of God's grace and love made to all who were willing to accept it. Citizenship in the kingdom of God could not be forced upon anyone but was open to all. "This kingdom," Jesus was saying, "is now at hand and open to all men who are ready to receive it." The whole purpose of his teaching and preaching was to open men's eyes to the reality of this kingdom, to outline to them the meaning of citizenship in it, and to urge them to prepare themselves for it. The kingdom of God was for all who were willing to penetrate its mysteries and to be transformed by them. At no time did Jesus make light of the fact that a radical change in life is involved for all who are interested in citizenship in the kingdom. It is so radical a change that John speaks of it as a rebirth; Paul speaks of it as becoming a new person, and it is clear from the New Testament records that only men of complete faith and in full obedience to Jesus Christ would think of seeking citizenship in that kingdom. Jesus referred to it as something that was within us and among us, but always as a gift of God's love and grace for all men. In the parables that deal with the kingdom he speaks of it in many ways: a tiny seed growing to a great tree, as leaven in a lump, as a priceless treasure hidden in the field.

Our Lord's preaching of the gospel of the kingdom of God provides a breathtaking vista of what life ought to be, of life as God intends it. And while many parts of it are baffling indeed, the main point is crystal-clear: if the purpose of our life is to become citizens of the kingdom of God, we must be willing to accept without question the leadership of Jesus Christ, to live the kind of life we see in him, and to do so no matter what the cost. This is the meaning of a Christian purpose in life.

We no sooner see it than we recognize the profound interplay between religion and life that goes on in such a purpose. Purpose binds life and faith together, and they must be kept together. Life divorced from faith is life without the power of a great purpose. Faith divorced from life is strictly irrelevant, useless, and not worth a moment's notice. The Christian faith talks about great goals and ideals; it speaks of the kingdom of God, of a new world in which peace and justice will rule. But these are simply vague sentiments and sweet words until and unless they are linked with life in a dynamic purpose. Life is a vast, chaotic jumble of problems that no one has an answer to unless men of great purpose set themselves to the task of bringing order out of the confusion.

A purpose, therefore, is more than an attitude, an idea, a sentiment; it is a plan of dedicated action, a course of committed conduct. What is more, a purpose is a commitment of life to certain ends. In early religion a holy purpose assumed before God was called a vow, a word made holy by God, and sanctified by the blessing of God himself, and a vow was not to be broken.

That, as I understand it, is what Jesus meant by an invitation to enter into the kingdom of God. To say "Yes" to this was to take a vow before God that would become the dominant purpose in life.

In the 1920's a group of learned Europeans tried to form what they called a League of Men of Goodwill, which they believed would be able to combat the rising tide of facism and communism that was battering down the ramparts of stability in Europe. All hail to their effort, even though it failed to achieve its purpose. But realistically it hadn't a chance of succeeding because it lacked spiritual power, rather, the power of a spiritual purpose. What is needed in the struggle for a Christian world order is not men of goodwill, but men of Christian purpose, men through whom the power of the Christian faith will flow into life, through whose purposes God's design brings order in man's disorder. And that is the

93

biggest and finally the only major task of this and the next generations.

One of my most hopeful experiences of the recent past was to share in the first interfaith conference on world peace to be held in this country. It was a thrilling experience to have Catholic, Jew, and Protestant stand side by side to think, pray, and plan for peace. It was a national conference in 1966, but it is growing like a mustard seed and has become a conference of world religions for peace. May God in his mercy bless this humble effort to find our way in his purpose!

III

We get some notion of the urgency of our search for fundamental order when we try to describe the day in which we live. We have heard it called a period of revolutionary change so frequently that the description has become trite. But sometimes I wonder whether the word "change" is as accurate as a more drastic word, "breakup." It seems to me that breakup is a truer way to describe what we are confronting today. Old philosophies of life, old ways of life, old understandings of the nature of the universe and man's capacity to do things, and most old religions have been torn and broken by some of the cruelest upheavals ever to rack human life and society.

This process of breakup has occurred on every continent, from pole to pole, and on every level of life. The world today presents a radically different prospect from the world of fifty years ago, and the change is far from being completed. Nor has this change been merely a matter of what has happened to states and in history. None of us have been spared, or will be spared, further breakups in our lives, whether we be farmer, factory worker, doctor, preacher, lawyer, or statesman. We all realize how radically different a world we live in from any we had planned.

In the Old Testament there is a poignant query which gives voice to what many of us are feeling: "If the foundations are destroyed, what can the righteous do?" (Psalms 11:3.) There may be some doubt as to whether we belong to the "righteous," but righteous or no, we live in a world whose foundations are being destroyed. And the young people of our time must frame their purpose, make their way, and live their lives in the most tumultuous world men have ever known.

Let the Italian movie producer speak of *Blow-Up* when he describes his young people. But my experience with the college generation leads me to a radically different conclusion. I find in them an unrelenting search for a great and honest purpose for life. Of course, they do not lack advice as to what purposes to serve. In fact, this very multiplicity of purposes may well give them their greatest problem. For champions of all the isms stand on every street corner today, seeking converts all along the line.

The February, 1967, issue of *Reader's Digest* carries

an article about Phillip Abbott Luce and his book *The New Left*. This is a vivid description of how a very gullible young man continued to be gullible all his life—and probably is as gullible today as ever he was. There is no reason to think he has learned very much from his experience of rapid and casual transfer from one ism to another. The one thing that is clear from his apologia is that he is still standing on street corners waiting for someone to give him a purpose for living. And he will not stand alone long before someone else comes along and does just this, and off he will go again.

Like their fathers before them, our young people may well begin as radicals, then become liberals, and finally, unless the grace of God protects them in an unusual way, end up being conservatives. While these are rather inexact tags, they do help us understand the differences in the purposes for which people live. A radical is one who accepts a breakup as good and proposes to carry it on until it is possible to make a really new start in human affairs. He not only welcomes change; he promotes and fosters it by fair means or foul—no matter who or how many get hurt—and usually he does what he does in the interests of some group. A liberal has been defined as a radical with a wife and two children! Be that as it may, he is usually inclined to move more deliberately toward goals that embrace the welfare of all. His methods will be those of persuasion rather than coercion, and he will try not to set group over against group in mortal conflict. The conservative, however defined, is one who seeks not only to arrest the disintegration of our tradition, but to strengthen it by all available means. That is his strength and his weakness. He is allergic to serious change and will not hesitate to control—stifle, if need be—all revolutionary movements in thought as well as action.

The Christian faith enters into competition with these and other purposes with the Christian purpose for life. It asks that our young people make this the purpose in their hearts lest they defile themselves. And, as you would suppose, the Christian purpose brings the eternal truth of the Christian faith to bear upon the problems that must be faced. And it brings with it the power of the greatest purpose known to man.

IV

What does it mean for us who aspire to be disciples of Jesus Christ today to take seriously the gospel of the kingdom of God for which he gave his life? A number of things seem to be quite clear. We will believe and be guided by certain convictions: (1) God is the Creator of life; (2) the will of God as we see it in Jesus Christ is to create the kingdom of love in the lives of men; (3) we are called to volunteer and to serve in that effort wherever the lines of our life take us.

As we look at these for a moment, we discover in them the framework of the kind of powerful Christian purpose that can give point and meaning to life. The Christian purpose is to work for the kind of society in which all men will know themselves to be and will indeed be recognized as the children of God and brothers of one another. This purpose becomes the *summum bonum,* the one great objective of our life. It is the end we are willing to seek with all our power, whether as teacher, preacher, lawyer, or doctor. The achievement of it calls for the shared efforts of all. It is not the obligation of any one profession or institution, but of all men wherever they work and live.

Lewis Mumford has written some of the finest interpretations of modern life that are available. I think so often of his description of the three requirements of a free society: communication, communion, and cooperation. I certainly do not want to dispute the value of these three or the fact that they are essentials of a Christian as well as a free society. But it does seem to me the Christian faith adds one thing to them—not so much another objective as an atmosphere in which the three he lists can really flourish: the atmosphere of love—love of God and love of man.

Every gardener knows that seeds which will flourish in one soil and climate will wilt and die in another. Just so, Mumford's objectives need the nourishment of love—a deep, all-inclusive love of God and man—if they are to flourish into a really free society. Only as they are a part of a purpose that is powered by the love of God as we find it in Christ, will they become effective principles of creative change and point the way toward new order in this day of mounting confusion.

V

Others may think—and properly so—of Columbus or Lincoln or William Lloyd Garrison when they think of the power of purpose in life, but I find myself thinking of John R. Mott, whose death some time ago reminded many of us of our indebtedness to him.

When John R. Mott graduated from Cornell University, he felt the call to Christian service in a needy world. He and some of his like-minded young friends organized the Student Volunteer Movement, which for fifty years encouraged the youth of Christian countries to accept the Christian purpose in their hearts and lives. Mott himself did this and picked as his special field the disorder and the separateness of the Christian churches. He felt it a sin and a shame that they were so far apart and without means even of communication with each other. He spent his entire life trying to bring them together in a meaningful way. That was the purpose of his life. That was his one message whenever he spoke. I recall hearing him while I was a freshman in Nebraska Wesleyan University in 1926 and again at the University of Chicago in 1933 and again in Atlanta in 1949, and he gave the same speech with the same sincerity and fervor on all three occasions. It was more than a good speech; it was a purpose incarnate in his life, and that made it a great speech.

Each one of us must ask himself whether he really wants to find and serve such a purpose. If this is our desire, there are several things that we must do.

99

We must find this purpose the same place Jesus Christ found it, namely in the will of God. For unless we can find the purpose of our lives in God's purpose for mankind, we shall not be dealing in the kind of ultimates that really give power to life.

We must believe in God and in his purpose flowing about us like the air, under us like the earth, in and through us like the germ plasm which unites the generations of men and from which we have been fashioned.

We must believe that in his purpose in our creation and nurture he has been bringing us to the edge of some great purpose that requires us—our minds, hearts, souls, strength—to seek a warm creative fellowship with one another and with him.

Above all, we must be willing to be led by him as he seeks to work in and through us. Worship, study, and the effort to understand him—all this, yes, but finally we must be willing to be obedient to him. This means that we shall have to learn how to be patient in the waiting (and there's much of that) as we seek some clue to his special purpose for us. We must be courageous in trying to follow where it seems to lead us. We must be humble enough to admit the misunderstandings and mistakes that we shall make as we seek to know and to serve him.

One thing is sure: we may fail with a purpose, but we cannot succeed without one. We may fail to build a Christian world, but we cannot even make a serious beginning toward it unless we have a devotion to the kingdom of God in our hearts—even as Jesus Christ did.

Years ago I ran across a poem that fastened itself on my mind:

> I hear about a man called Jesus
>   Who went about doing good.
> It troubles me that I am so easily content
>   With just going about.

John R. Mott heard about a man called Jesus Christ who believed in the kingdom of God and who went about doing good in behalf of that kingdom. It troubled John R. Mott too, and he purposed in his heart to follow where his Master led. And so can we, so must we, if we are willing to accept the mantle of discipleship in the service of Jesus Christ.

7. He Cleansed the Temple

Scripture: *Mark 11:15-19; John 2:13-22*

I

The cleansing of the temple is one of the best attested, most striking, and most misunderstood deeds of Jesus Christ. How shall we think of it? Why did he do it? Was he but a spiritual forerunner of the pathetic Don Quixote, who roamed Spain jousting at windmills? Or could this particular deed be "a moment in the conscience of man" when even our most sacred institutions are brought before the bar of judgment? If the temple of his day needed cleaning, what shall we say of the church today? Does she not need it too? These and other questions stand for answer as we probe the event itself.

This particular deed made so deep an impression on the early Christians that it appears in all four Gospels. Mark, the first one to be written, and John, the latest, have the fullest accounts of it. Matthew and Luke list but do not dwell on it. Interesting similarities and in some cases puzzling differences occur in the four accounts of it.

All agree that it took place; John places it very early in the public ministry, while the other three place it late—on Monday of our Lord's final week on earth. John, seeing in it our Lord's break with the externalism of faith at the very opening of his ministry, follows it with the stories of Nicodemus and the woman at the well of Samaria—both of which stress the spiritual nature of true worship, saying in effect that whenever men worship God in spirit and in truth, whether in the temple or elsewhere, they are in the presence of God himself.

Matthew, Mark, and Luke see in the event a decisive turn in our Lord's relationship with the religious leaders of his people, who had had him under surveillance for some time. They were well aware of his sharp attacks upon the externalism of their understanding of religion. They knew he posed a real threat to their understanding of the primacy of the Law and the temple. While they had warned him repeatedly and most solemnly, they had made no real move to silence him. Whatever question they may have had about how to deal with him was answered by this event. Luke puts it simply: "The chief priests and the scribes and the principal men of the people sought to destroy him." Apparently this action sealed his fate as far as they were concerned.

The event itself is not difficult to describe or to understand. Jesus and his disciples had come to Jerusalem with every Jew who could make it to celebrate the week-long feast of the Passover. The city overflowed with pilgrims on such occasions, with the multitude who found sleeping places outside the city, coming to the temple early in the morning and spending the day sharing in the services of worship. Placed on the highest promontory, resplendent with marble and gold, the temple was so beautiful that a proverb of that day ran, "You have not seen anything beautiful until you see Herod's Temple." It was the center of Israel's life as a people of God. "The sanctity of the Temple was unique" in that for seven hundred years "only there could sacrifices be offered in obedience to the Law." [1] Devout Jews either brought the required offerings with them or bought them after they arrived. Obviously it would be most difficult for a Jew living in Tarsus, hundreds of miles away, to bring a live animal by sea or on a pack train to Jerusalem for sacrifice. Hence the temple authorities had made provision whereby such pilgrims might purchase proper animals and fowls after they arrived at the temple.

In addition to the tax every Jew had to pay to the temple, offerings might be made in coin, but the coins could have no image on them. Thus Roman coins, bearing the image of Caesar, had to be exchanged for ceremonially acceptable ones as soon as the pilgrim arrived in the temple, much as we change our money into the currency of the lands we visit today. Temple authorities

[1] Madeleine S. Miller and J. Lane Miller, *Harper's Bible Dictionary* (New York: Harper & Brothers, 1952), p. 731.

104

had made provision for this exchange by licensing money changers and giving them space in the temple area.

Mark intimates that a regular road ran from the shops of the city through the outer court to the gates that led north and south of the temple area, making of it a literal thoroughfare during the festivals.

So during the Passover the temple was like nothing else on earth. It was a thoroughfare, a stockyard, a slaughterhouse, a pen for fowls, and stalls for money changers with the men who ran each business pushing their own trade as hard as they could. The oriental bazaars of our time come the closest to paralleling what must have been the situation in the temple on that fateful day when Jesus and his followers set about cleansing it. Whatever else it was, the temple was not a house of prayer, a place of worship!

Just why the contradiction between the purpose for which the temple was built and the practices being pursued in it hit him so hard upon this occasion, we will never know. He had been in the temple on holy days many times, yet never before had he been moved to action by the contradiction he found there. But never before had he come to Jerusalem and the temple with so keen a consciousness that God had set him apart to preach the kingdom of God and to call all men into it. His disappointment over the negative response of the religious leaders to his message must have been hard to bear. They had completely missed the point of what he said in their preoccupation with the externals of faith —with the proper offerings, the proper garments, and

105

the proper prayers. They had strained at a gnat and swallowed a camel! They had polished the outside of the cup but neglected the inside of it.

Here they were at it again, ignoring God and honoring themselves! On this great festival set apart to celebrate the holiness and goodness of God, in this sacred place set apart for a thousand years for the worship of God, the raucous roar of the road, the marketplace, and the bazaar drowned out the calls to prayer even then being lifted by the Levites in the court of priests!

Something snapped in his system of restraints. He could take it no longer! He grabbed up a handful of reeds used to bed the cattle and began to drive the animals out of the court. His followers must have lent an enthusiastic hand because in a twinkling chaos descended on the bazaar. Cattle and sheep were being loosed from their pens and driven outside the wall; owners of birds were warned to get them out of the temple; money changers had their tables of coins upset, and people came running from all directions. The priests, who had licensed the shopkeepers, came too and demanded to know by what authority Jesus was doing all this. The answer he gave was drawn from the prophets: "Is it not written, 'My house shall be called a house of prayer for all the nations'? [Isaiah 56:7] But you have made it a den of robbers" [Jeremiah 7:11]. He charged them with profaning the holy place; he took upon himself the responsibility of cleansing the temple, and that is just what he did!

106

II

Jesus was far from being alone in his love of the temple as the place where men came to worship God in the beauty of holiness. As a boy he had learned and as a man he had found the deep truth of "the supreme temple psalm," written hundreds of years before by one who like him knew the purpose of the holy place:

> How lovely is thy dwelling place,
>   O Lord of hosts!
> My soul longs, yea, faints
> for the courts of the Lord;
> my heart and flesh sing for joy
>   to the living God.
>
> Even the sparrow finds a home,
>   and the swallow a nest for herself,
>   where she may lay her young,
> at thy altars, O Lord of hosts,
>   my king and my God.
> Blessed are those who dwell in thy house,
>   ever singing thy praise! . . .
>
> For a day in thy courts is better
>   than a thousand elsewhere.
> I would rather be a doorkeeper in the house of
>   my God
>   than dwell in the tents of wickedness.
>
> PSALMS 84:1-4, 10

Nor was Jesus the first to protest the abuses of the temple. The prophets before him had done this. When

107

the armies of the Greek conquerors had profaned the temple by offering unclean animals on the altar, Judas Maccabeus dismantled the altar piece by piece and purified every single stone before rebuilding it. And the people who wrote and treasured the Dead Sea Scrolls were so offended by the worldliness of the temple and the priests that they refused even to enter the place! One of the works of the expected Messiah was to cleanse the temple and recenter the life of Israel there in the adoration of God.

Though the Hebrews had built at least three temples on the same high place at great cost of time, money, and labor, they discovered—as men of faith all do—that it is far, far easier to build a temple than it is to keep it clean. Not physically clean, but clean in the biblical sense: aware of the purpose, loyal to the purpose, fulfilling the purpose for which it was built. For the most important thing about a temple is not the material out of which it is built nor the lines and colors of its structure, but the intention, the purpose, the reason for its being. And when what goes on in the temple does not serve this basic purpose, the temple is profaned by it, and must be cleansed of it. That, I am sure, is why Jesus did what he did on that fateful day.

III

The incident has been radically misunderstood, and I must say it does lend itself to some misunderstanding. I myself shared in a small way in one such misunderstanding many years ago. In the turbulent days before we became involved in World War II, I was a member of a small group appearing before the Foreign Relations Committee of the Senate in opposition to one of the steps we were taking that seemed to be leading us directly into the war itself. Our group was being criticized by some members of the Committee for our pacifism. One of them went so far as to say that it was unchristian to be a pacifist and cited what Jesus did with the whip to prove that righteous people must upon occasion use force against evildoers. It was painful to point out that the whip was no whip in the ordinary sense and that it was not used on men but was in literal fact a handful of rushes snatched from the ground and used to drive the animals out of the court. There were certain other difficulties with the analogy, but I did not press them because I felt sure than no one was really listening to what we were saying.

But we must not let such misuses of the incident blind us to the enduring insights it provides those who will pause to study it. The most obvious one is this: we need and must have places of worship, and we must be vigilant to maintain them as places of worship, suggesting and nurturing a kind of creative openness to God as the Lord of life. Yet to have a temple or a church is to venture into the risky waters of institutionalism. For a church means a building, a program of services, and many kinds of activities, a corps of leaders, boards, commissions, committees, and—inescapably—a budget! Inevitably, a church develops a tradition of belief and practice celebrated in creed and sacrament in which the cumulative experiences of succeeding generations find expression. The older the church, the more fixed the tradition becomes, and soon the church will be tempted to call into leadership those who not only love God and the church, but who also love the church as it is, the tradition as it is, the rites and ceremonies as they are, the program as it is. The educational efforts of the institution will begin to spend more and more time interpreting the tradition and the institution and less and less time in a creative openness to God, which is what worship really is.

If history is to be believed, there is a wide gate and a broad way that leads from public worship to institutionalism, to externalism, and finally to the perversion of the very meaning of the worship of God into the worship of the church. And in the last stages men will exclaim over the beauty of the building rather than be overwhelmed by the beauty of holiness in the sanctuary. Then, if the church is to live as a church and not as a museum, comes the moment of cleansing and renewal in which the church rededicates herself to her purpose and calling.

There is no easy way for the church to become, to be, and to continue as the church, as the point at which men in need discover the One who is sufficient for every human need. But it must be done today as it has always been done in the past, by those who love the Lord of the church and see in this all-too-human institution an opportunity to know God better and to serve him more faithfully.

I beg of you, even as I remind myself: do not love any church because of the beauty of her structure and line or the richness of her program or the number and status of her members, but love the church for God's sake— and his alone!

IV

The cleansing of the temple illustrates an interesting fact about sincere prophetic critics of religious institutions: there comes a time when they must move from word to deed to creative rebellion. Had the prophets before Jesus and Jesus himself been content to let the matter end with reasoned criticism of what they felt to be wrong, they would have been spared the lethal retaliation of those they criticized. But when they made the move against existing custom and policy, the die was cast. Jeremiah went into the well by royal edict and Jesus went to the cross.

Yet such men must make their move in order to keep faith with their divine call. The prophets of ancient Israel—Elijah, for example—had to move against such kings and queens as Ahab and Jezebel. The Christian leaders in the Roman world had to move against the Roman edicts which required them to worship the emperor. Luther struggled for years to be a faithful son of Rome, yet the time finally came when in fidelity to his call to criticize the existing church he had to move —and how he moved!

It was so with John Wesley and the Church of England. He loved that church with a love that never

111

THE DEEDS OF CHRIST

ended. He valued his orders in her ministry so highly that he never surrendered them, not even when the doors of her churches were closed to him and his movement. But John Wesley could no more deny the imperious call of the Holy Spirit to leave the peaceful confines of those churches and preach the gospel to all men than he could stop breathing. His criticisms—once words—became deeds, deeds that with an inner logic of their own led him farther and farther away from the established church of his time. The word had to become the deed, had to take on the flesh of action, if it were to be true to itself.

Much early Methodist history clusters around the tip of Manhattan in old John Street Church, an interesting and vital repository of historic faith. But no part of that story better deserves the telling today than something that happened there in the 1840's. The Negroes were flocking into the Methodist movement in the North and the South alike. In the South they were slaves, and the churches reflected that fact. While technically free in the North, they were treated like slaves—made to sit in the balcony, eat at separate tables, and denied full equality in conference discussion and placement, etc. They objected to this in the name of their common faith, but their objections were passed over with familiar words, "Now don't push too hard; just take your time. Things will work out all right." But there came a time when the Negro members of The Methodist Church said, "Either we stay as equals or we leave and form a church of our own," and they left and formed the African Methodist Episcopal Church, which today ministers to far more Negroes than does The United Methodist Church. As we think of the reunion of the various Methodist bodies in this country, we meet head-on the initial reason why they left and formed a church of their own. They want the answer to one question: Do we come together as equals? That is more than a question; it is a criticism; it is more than a criticism; it is an act—both explicit and implicit.

Bishop James Pike gets a mixed but interested press among churchmen these days. Yet in him I see a continuation of this ancient tradition of prophetic protest. His criticisms of the church have been unsparing, firm, and out in the open for twenty years or more. They were heard, tolerated, and generally ignored by churchmen. Finally, in fidelity to what he believed to be the intellectual integrity of the Christian tradition, his criticism passed over into certain formal challenges to historic beliefs. When rebuffed and asked in effect to keep silence, he demanded public trial. There can be no denying his proper place in the historic tradition of those who reach a moment in their relationship with an institution where inner restraints snap and criticism moves from word to deed.

There comes a time when this must happen, when creative criticism must move from word to deed or die. Many of our thoughtful young college leaders are beginning to ignore the local churches in this country, and by doing this they criticize the church. They are not atheists, though they demand the right to know the meaning of the God-is-dead theology. They are not moral

113

derelicts, though they demand to know the reasons behind existing moral codes, and they claim the right to move in new directions if this seems to be best. They are not antichurch, but they cannot endure the humdrum irrelevance of most local churches. They are not socially irresponsible; they want to be involved in the grave issues of our time; they want to take up the cause of our commonly accepted preachments of brotherhood, justice, and peace and do something about them. They want to pass from word to deed, from resolution to demonstration, from groups for reasoning to groups for sharing.

We ought to be proud of them; we ought to let them know of our confidence in them even if we take sedation in order to sleep some nights. They are not making any more trouble for us than we made for our fathers, and they are making the right kind of trouble.

They are trying to cleanse the church of irrelevance, or excessive preoccupation with form, liturgy, tradition, and playing it cool on hot issues. They want to be, and they want the church to be, "where the action is." Of late I have shared in many discussions and debates on college and university campuses on the issues of the war in Vietnam, and I know how deeply and sincerely concerned our most thoughtful students are about this tangled and troubled situation. Whatever else we may call them, they will never be called the "let well enough alone" generation, the "play it cool" generation, the "let nature take her course" generation. Something has snapped within their system of restraints, and they are moving into the area of decisive action on this and other matters. But let none of us, regardless of how we judge what they do, think that they are the first to leave the safe harbor of criticism and move into the stormy sea of deeds. They may do more than save themselves; they may yet save the church from the worst of all possible fates: an honored position on the sidelines of the hard game of ethical and moral living.

V

One of the most profound lines in the many books of Harry Emerson Fosdick is this: "All reformation is restoration." [2] He is writing of the direction of the thrust of the prophets in Israel's life, but his insight throws light on what Jesus and other creative rebels have done, and it suggests a basic understanding of creative criticism and rebellion in all generations.

Rebels, like Jesus, seek the reformation of the temple, not its demolition. They are trying to put piorities in perspective once more, to put first things first. They all reach a certain point—God alone knows where it is or why they reach it when they do—when the inner restraints snap and they move into open rebellion against existing structures.

The fundamental revolutions they usher in are as much recovery of the old as exploration of the new. For them the God of yesterday is the Lord of today and of tomorrow as well, and they trust his leading. This we

[2] A *Guide to Understanding the Bible* (New York: Harper & Brothers, 1938), p. 99.

need to keep in mind as we take our stand in the Christian church today. At the heart of our tradition is a *person*—a young man who lived close to God and close to man, whose love for God included and gave content to his love for man, whose love for the Lord of the temple kept temple procedures in perspective, who moved from word to deed at the behest of God himself. When this young man felt that God wanted him to say something, he said it, or to do something, he did it. There comes a time when the church like her Lord must leave the quiet life of accepting existing patterns to preach the gospel on the highways of the world and finally be willing to try to cleanse the temple of irrelevance, ease, and simple lack of concern.

I do not think it irrelevant for us to take to ourselves the explanation he made to those who demanded to know why he did what he did: "My Father is working still, and I am working."

8. He Stood Trial Four Times

Scripture: *Matthew 26:57-66; 27:1-2, 11-26*

I

Most of us will never have to stand trial for any reason. Some of us may have one or more brushes with the event during our entire lifetime. But few if any of us will ever be on trial for our lives, and our legal system explicitly prevents our being tried for the same capital offense four times over, as Jesus was.

Anyway we look at it, a trial is a frightening thing. It is a point at which the collective judgment of society in the form of law is focused on an individual who is charged with violating it. His status in society—perhaps his very life and freedom—are at stake. If he is declared innocent, society grants him absolution, and all is as nearly well as could be after sustained public exposure. If he is declared guilty, society continues to bring its judgment to bear upon him in the form of penalties of one kind or another.

As we move the focus of our study of the deeds of Christ to the last week of his life, we come to his arrest and trials. It is not necessary to dwell on the details of this shame-filled episode. We know them well enough.

He was arrested by soldiers from the temple late Thursday night following his final supper with his disciples and taken to the home of the high priest for interrogation. His disciples, excepting Peter and possibly one other, had fled as the arrest was being made. A strong tradition credits Peter with staying close to him all that evening and night until he was forced into a denial of ever having known him.

But what about four trials? I must hasten to say that I am not sure there were four authentic trials; in fact, I am not sure there was even one such! But there were a number of hearings before officers of the law, hearings that added momentum to the move that was to result in his crucifixion. Therefore we will not be far wrong if we think of one hearing occurring on Thursday night and two trials on Friday morning, interrupted by a hearing before Herod. Next came the sentence of death and the legally prescribed flogging by Pilate, then the Via Dolorosa and the crucifixion.

The shame of it all overwhelms us as we seek to reconstruct the event from the scanty records at hand. We have no records, either Jewish or Roman, from outside the New Testament tradition that throw more light on that tradition. In the Four Gospels themselves we meet much confusion and some actual contradiction in chronology and detail. Though scholars have been trying to unravel the mystery of these records for hundreds of years, the task remains unfinished. We ought to be eternally grateful to them for throwing as much light as they have on the reasons behind the differences in the Gospels. One fact stands out: all Gospels agree that Jesus was arrested, given short hearings before Jewish and Roman authorities, found guilty on a trumped-up charge, and executed by Roman order and Roman soldiers.

But the question still persists: Did he ever have a fair trial? There is no reason why he should not have had one. Two sets of law, Jewish and Roman, were focused on him at that time. Two courts, Jewish and Roman, were at hand to conduct such a trial, and each court was presided over by an officer who had much experience in conducting such trials. Strange, is it not, that he may never have had one?

I neglected to mention a third kind of law that was abundantly present—lynch law, and the excitable crowd under the firm control of its leaders—these too were a decisive factor in the events that brought the public ministry of Jesus to its tragic yet triumphant climax.

II

Skipping over the shadowy details of the arrest and hearing on Thursday night, the Gospels, with the exception of John, picture him as being brought before the

Sanhedrin, the highest official Jewish court, shortly after dawn on Friday.

This court was composed of seventy-one persons: the chief priests of the temple; the elders of Israel, that is, representatives of the oldest and most respected families in Jerusalem; and the scribes and Pharisees who represented the puritanical tradition in Judaism. The Sanhedrin was presided over by the high priest himself, Caiaphas on this occasion. Twenty-three members of the court could form a quorum. A bare majority of one could acquit, and a majority of two could convict. During the Greek and Roman periods it was the supreme council and high court of justice in Jerusalem. It was a political assembly as well as a court of law. Its members could hear and hand down binding decisions on all sorts of cases, ranging from treason to divorce and blasphemy. Over the three hundred years of its existence it had built up a formidable mass of precedents and was openly jealous of the rights of the accused. Its trial of Jesus was highly irregular—almost as much as the one which preceded the stoning of Stephen and the near lynching of Paul at a later date. Despite such lapses, we get some notion of the stability of this court from the fact that once Rome became acquainted with its role in Israel's life, she gladly turned over to it the large majority of disputes that arose among the Jewish people, reserving always for herself the right to pass and inflict the death penalty.

The members of the Sanhedrin who heard the questioning of Jesus that Friday morning were among the most highly respected leaders of his people; they were trained in the law; they were accustomed to hearing trials and making decisions. They stood in a long and honorable tradition that prized justice and fairness for the accused.

It is difficult to get a clear notion of what actually went on in this trial. Caiaphas seems to have questioned Jesus briefly about two matters: what he had said about the temple and whether he thought himself to be the Messiah, as his followers were claiming.

Had he, in fact, threatened to destroy the temple and then rebuild it? Witnesses were introduced, but they disagreed on what he had said about this so the charge was dropped and never brought up again.

Was he the Messiah? As Mark tells the story, "Again the high priest asked him, 'Are you the Christ, the Son of the Blessed?' And Jesus said, 'I am; and you will see the Son of man sitting at the right hand of Power, and coming with the clouds of heaven.' And the high priest tore his mantle, and said, 'Why do we still need witnesses? You have heard his blasphemy. What is your decision?' And they all condemned him as deserving death." Matthew and Luke lend substantial agreement to this description though John furnishes a quite different account of the entire trial.

There is essential agreement in the records on the fact that very early on Friday morning, having reached a decision, the officers of the Sanhedrin hurried Jesus to Pilate's court. Some scholars think that Pilate must have been alerted by Jewish authorities that they were going to arrest Jesus and bring him in for trial. In any event, Pilate was waiting for them. The mob, smelling blood, had begun to gather as Jesus was brought to the Sanhedrin and Pilate's court.

The trouble we have had reconstructing a clear story of events up to this point is as nothing when compared with the trouble we meet as we try to determine what actually went on in the trial before Pilate. All four Gospels agree that the Jewish authorities brought Jesus to Pilate asking the death penalty on the charge of potential insurrection. The records agree that Pilate knew at once that Jesus was innocent of the charge of subversion and insurrection, or plotting the overthrow of Caesar and declaring himself an earthly king. All agree that Pilate tried to free Jesus but was deterred by the warnings of the priests and the howls of the mob. When Pilate offered to free either Jesus or Barabbas, a common murderer, the mob chose Barabbas. When Pilate asked what they wanted him to do with Jesus, they answered instantly, "Crucify him."

Pilate stalled for time by sending Jesus across the city to be interviewed and possibly tried and sentenced by Herod, who ruled Galilee and therefore possessed authority over Galileans if he chose to assume it. But if he did not want to assume it, then Pilate as the ruler in Jerusalem had to take it. The priests and the mob trailed along on the journey from Pilate to Herod and repeated their accusations of the Galilean. Herod could not have cared less about the substance of the dispute. He wanted a miracle and asked for one, but Jesus was in no mood to entertain royalty just then so he said and did nothing. Herod, in high good humor because of the recognition by Pilate, had Jesus arrayed in royal purple and taken back to Pilate as though he were a king! Pilate dallied no longer; about nine o'clock in the morning he washed his hands of the whole affair and pronounced the death sentence. He flogged Jesus as required by law and turned him over to the crucifixion detail of the Roman guards.

Though the driving force of the entire proceeding was the determination of the leaders of his own people to have him decisively put out of the way, though the shouts of the mob of his own people finally firmed Pilate's decision to do just that, it was by Roman order he went to his death on a Roman cross put there by Roman soldiers. But the Jewish authorities who had arrested him in the garden never left his side, even going with him to Calvary, where some mocked his agony.

III

We turn away from all this, torn between rage, tears, and prayers. No other story I know moves me so deeply. It may not be possible for me or anyone nurtured on these stories from earliest infancy to be objective about this succession of events, but we must make the effort, and as we do, certain insights take shape.

The first is a new awareness of how desperately difficult it is to try to administer justice in a time of maximum or critical tension. It is hard enough to get at the right and wrong of rumors and charges in a relatively calm situation.

Some weeks ago I read Judge David Peck's masterly reconstruction of the famous Greer case that occupied so much attention here in New York City and in Boston twenty years ago. As I read it, I marveled at the patience and skill with which the case was handled by the attorneys and the judge. While interest was high, no mobs gathered outside to complicate matters. In the case of still another trial, involving Henry Ward Beecher, prominent Brooklyn preacher of Civil War days, we encounter a much more critical situation from the point of view of public interest. He was being tried as an adulterer in what came to be one of the most famous lawsuits of the nineteenth century. Feelings ran high, yet counsel for both sides went about their work with great care, seeking justice.

Louis Nizer's book *The Jury Returns* reminds laymen in the law, like myself, of the infinite patience which is essential to the achievement of justice, even today in a relatively quiet setting.

When the nazi leaders were brought before the Nuremberg tribunal, the furious emotions of the war were still raging. Yet the jurists tried to be fair, and did so in an amazing way. One of the alternate judges in the American delegation to the trial was John Parker of Charlotte, North Carolina, the presiding judge in the circuit court of appeals in that area. When Judge Parker returned, he told some of us of the trial. One interesting item in that recital stuck in my memory. When the

124

justices of the victorious nations met to outline the procedures for the trial, the leader of the Russian group was quite impatient over the time he saw being consumed by the careful procedures under discussion. He said, "Why take so much time for this? Let's give them a fair trial and shoot them!"

Let any situation heat up, let the mobs form, let fear begin to stalk the land, let self-righteous anger begin to blind men's eyes and twist men's judgments, and the administration of justice becomes infinitely complicated. It should not, but it does. For judges and rulers like Caiaphas and Pilate are human. They have ears; they can hear the mob. They have normal ambitions for security and advancement; they want to quell criticism and challenges to their competence. As long as human beings like us—and Caiaphas and Pilate—are the men who must act as judges, we shall be appalled at the ease with which men in power will in the name of prudence actually and frequently subvert the law's intention to administer justice.

I ask you, should not an innocent man go free? The answer is an unqualified "Yes." But is it really unqualified? Ought we not say, "Yes, unless a mob is howling for the blood of the accused; then he may be punished as though guilty as charged"!

Even Pilate, hardened Roman procurator that he was, seems to have been troubled by the decision to execute Jesus. In a gesture that will be associated with his name as long as it persists in human history, he "took water and washed his hands before the crowd, saying, 'I am

125

innocent of this man's blood; see to it yourselves.' " The people accepted this awful responsibility with great gusto, "His blood be on us and on our children!"—an ancient way of accepting tribal responsibility for the deed they were about to do.

Thus Pilate like Lady Macbeth thought to wash his guilt away, but he found as did she that no amount of hand washing will remove such "damned spots"; the creeds of Christendom give the lie to Pilate's hope, for we say of Jesus Christ, "He suffered under Pontius Pilate, was crucified. . . ."

IV

Another insight furnished by these hearings and trials of our Lord is the ease with which we lose sight of the main issues in such a situation. In the trial of Socrates, three hundred years earlier, the Athenian judges lost sight of justice to the man. In Jesus' trial justice to the Galilean was the issue, but neither Caiaphas nor Pilate nor the Sanhedrin nor the mob could keep it uppermost in their minds. Their fear of criticism let them hear only the roar of the mob, which grew louder and louder until it dominated the scene and dictated the verdict.

Ironically, through it all the victims had a childlike faith in the truth of their cases. In Plato's *Apology* Socrates says, "My only eloquence lies in the truth!" He was willing to let truth plead his case, he said. Well, he did and he died. So also with Jesus. He said he had come to bear witness to the truth. Pilate interrupted scornfully, "What is truth?"—and Jesus died.

History warns us not to expect too much of ourselves in critical situations. It seems almost beyond our power to keep the main issues in focus in a time of crisis and great fear.

We well remember being gripped by one form of mass hysteria after another during and after both world wars. Can any who lived through it ever forget the way we treated our Japanese-American citizens immediately after Pearl Harbor? They were hustled out of their homes and places of business, herded into parks and stadiums, surrounded by armed guards, and treated as enemy aliens. And all this without the semblance of a hearing, a trial, or any other administration of justice and law. We would rather not remember the question a crying boy put to his father as they were being hauled out of their home: "What have we done?" Even though we tried to make amends, the damage was done; and we learned then that like any other people we can, do, and probably will lose our heads and compromise our judgments in time of grave crisis. It is a sobering thing to realize that the mass man in each of us reaches out for the security, the anonymity, and the power of the mob man we can so easily become.

Red-hunting has been the favorite indoor sport since 1920 in the United States, and there are many who still live by and for it. As long as we have the House Committe on Un-American Activities and believe the

127

vicious and unsubstantiated charges it makes against fellow Americans, the witch-hunting will continue.

I think of Louis Nizer's gripping description of the case of John Henry Faulk. It reminds us how ominously easy it is for a man to be blacklisted without any real evidence, solely through the power of innuendo, the big-lie technique, and outright intimidation.

Colleges and universities recall with a shudder the nightmare of the early 1950's when Senator Joseph Mc-Carthy was riding high. Since I was closely related to three of the institutions which rejected his offer to purge their faculties of Communists and Communist sympathizers, I recall the era with great feeling. The reaction of the senator's friends to these refusals was instant and unqualified: "What are you trying to hide?" they demanded to know. It was almost futile to point out that the trustees and the administrations of the universities in question were charged by law with the responsibility of guiding the policies of the universities and needed no help from the senator and his entourage in doing it.

The churches have felt and continue to feel in a lessening degree the heat of this Red-hunting mania. And not a few sober, thoughtful people have been troubled by it, thinking, "Where there's so much smoke there must be some fire." Along with some of the really choice spirits in our churches—in whose company I take humble delight—I found myself listed in the "pink fringe," a list of "suspicious churchmen" drawn up by the circuit riders, a group of laymen who were properly and sincerely alarmed at the thought that the faith was being betrayed by the infiltration of the clergy and church groups by Communist ideology. I was shocked to find my name in that list but was immediately reassured by the company I was in: most of the bishops of The Methodist Church, everyone connected with the Methodist Federation for Social Action, and anyone who was a member of the F.O.R. or any other group working for social reform. Finally, it became so much a badge of honor to be in the book that when upon one occasion they neglected to list me, I wrote and asked to be reinstated because I would rather face the questions that came from being included in the list than those that came from being excluded!

This little group of "circuit riders" (they have profaned a historic Methodist name) continues in a diminishing way to launch scare campaigns whenever it is known that anyone on their list is going to appear to speak in any given locality in the central South and in certain states in the North. They launch attacks upon the Revised Standard Version of the Bible, the National Council of Churches, the World Council of Churches, and any group that will not be intimidated into silence by their threats of "exposure."

All these situations—now so much a part, or a recent part, of our living experience—remind us of the difficulty of keeping an eye on the main issues of justice, truth, and love in any controversial situation.

V

While many other things might be said about the hearings and trials of our Lord, one fact seems to stand out at least equal to, if not above, all the others: the issue in any trial of a human being, whether formal or informal, is or ought to be *that human being*, the way in which truth and justice are focused by human beings on the life of this person. If in the pursuit of a principle, however exhalted, we lose sight of the person, however humble, if in the service of a legal principle, we lose sight of our human responsibilities to the enduring ideals of justice and truth as they bear on the life of one human being, a grave injustice to this human being is in the making and will certainly take place. The achievement of justice actually begins where a trial begins—in the heart, mind, and judgment of all concerned people. Justice can be served properly only as it is desired and treasured by the individual members of the group.

I find myself more and more inclined toward the position that the pursuit of truth and justice as they apply to a human being is possible only if conducted by and in the spirit of love for that and every other human being. We cannot deal with men as though they were items or numbers. They are persons and deserve to be dealt with in a spirit of love and understanding. Only then can we ignore the mobs and the clamor of our fears and deal with every man as he must be dealt with finally—as a child of the living God and deserving of every understanding and manifestation of mercy, compassion, and brotherhood. In the trial of Jesus Christ we meet more than Pilate and Caiaphas and their weaknesses. We meet ourselves and our weaknesses, ourselves and our opportunities to serve God more faithfully in the day in which we live.

9. He Forgave His Enemies

Scripture: *Matthew 5:38-48; Luke 23:26-48*

Text: *Father, forgive them; for they know not what they do.*

I

No part of the Sermon on the Mount sounds stranger to our ears than the advice: "Love your enemies and pray for those who persecute you." This is so astounding, so shocking to common sense, that we have tried to dismiss it as the counsel of perfection suitable perhaps for a never-never world but certainly not to be taken seriously in this world. Yet this ancient and massive evasion has failed us utterly for a number of reasons.

First, the advice belongs where we find it in that sermon. It is an integral part of what Jesus was saying to his disciples. Take it out, and a yawning gap exists in the structure of his thought. He was telling his disciples about the kingdom of God and the meaning of citizenship in it. He had spoken of the various dangers they must overcome if they were to become such citizens: greed, fear, lust. Next he had to speak of hate and how to overcome it.

There is a second reason why we cannot turn away from this advice: it is the simple fact that he clearly intends his disciples to take it seriously and to live by it. What we might want to dismiss as perfectionist, he advances as practical and essential to a life of faith and witness.

A final reason why we must say "Yes" or "No" to this staggering admonition is that he himself said "Yes" to it and actually put it into practice. It was startling enough to hear him say at the opening of his ministry, "Love your enemies and pray for those who persecute you," but it is little less than overwhelming to hear those very first words from the cross confirm this faith, "Father, forgive them; for they know not what they do."

We may say, as I suppose most of us would, that we cannot love our enemies and pray for those who persecute us, but we must not say that it cannot be done. He did it, and what is more, he expected his followers to do it too.

To those who think this line of thought an adventure in pious irrelevance, I suggest that it points an answer to the deepest moral struggle of our time, one on which the actual continuation of life on this planet may well be turning. We must conquer enmity and hate or perish; that is clear, and that is the main issue before us now. Yet wars and threats of war and all forms of civil strife grow out of injury and injustice, fancied or real. How are we to deal with these evils, these seedbeds of hate in our common life? That is the question to which two dramatically opposing answers are now being given: retaliation and reconciliation. When I say that the spirit and example of Jesus Christ opts for reconciliation, I am not denying for a moment that there is ample scriptural warrant for retaliation.

We find at least the spirit of retaliation in Paul's letter to the Romans. He recognizes the revolutionary nature of the Christian ethic and yet he writes, "Repay no one evil for evil, ... Never avenge yourselves, but leave it to the wrath of God; . . . . 'If your enemy is hungry, feed him; if he is thirsty, give him drink; for by so doing you will heap burning coals upon his head.' "

Somehow I cannot imagine our Lord ever saying that. To be quite candid about it Paul is advocating a sophisticated and pious form of retaliation. He certainly wants someone—God, to be explicit—to punish his enemies in such a way that they will not forget it and be brought to a feeling of repentance by it!

No, Jesus was going in a quite different direction in his thought on how to deal with injury and injustice. He was seeking reconciliation, an actual healing of an actual breach, among men, and he thought the only proper place to begin was with an unconditional forgiveness of any and all who might wrong us.

HE FORGAVE HIS ENEMIES

But can this be done? Isn't it expecting too much of poor, finite, fallible, groping, scarcely-out-of-the-jungle beings like us? Here again we can only say in general terms: he thought not; he really expected that we would measure up if we would follow him.

II

Our Lord's thought on this matter of forgiveness begins with his conviction that God forgives the sins of men and does so because of his steadfast love and determination to have man in a relationship of trust and faith with himself. Jesus is not trying to evade the problem of evil and sin; he is grappling with it in the spirit of the God he seeks to serve. He stands in a tradition which has emphasized the spirit of forgiveness in one way or another almost from its inception.

It will help us understand our present moral obligation if we take a careful look at the development of the idea of forgiveness in Hebrew and early Christian thought.

One of the oldest problems man has had to face is the one we are considering: What is the proper reaction to someone who has injured you? Within the span of human experience recorded in the Bible four major answers have emerged.

The first is unlimited vengeance. I know of no better statement of this answer than that found in Lamech's warning to his hearers:

THE DEEDS OF CHRIST

> I have slain a man for wounding me,
>   a young man for striking me.
> If Cain is avenged sevenfold,
>   truly Lamech seventy-sevenfold.
>   GENESIS 4:23-24

This obviously is the ethical credo of barbarism. It recognizes no limit to the vengeance you can wreak upon someone who has injured you. You are entitled to take his life, the life of his family and tribe, his possessions, his burial ground, his god, his sacred places, and erase them from life and the face of the earth.

Unlimited vengeance is not merely the belief of the historic stage of civilization called barbarism; it is the belief of the barbarian in every man, even sophisticated modern man. It is the sentiment which writes this poem that comes from the heart of the Jews of central Europe, suffering as they have seldom suffered in their long and tragic history:

> This time we shall not forgive—
> This time we shall not stretch our hand
> And offer "peace" to our foes.
> This time we shall build a raging fire
> Unquenchable
> Eternal
> Upon the altar of our heart!
> This time we shall not forget! [1]

The next answer to the problem of how to deal with injury and injustice is considerably higher in the scale

[1] Paul Eldridge, *Opinion*, 1946.

of morality than unlimited vengeance and might be called limited vengeance. This is the virtue extolled in the book of Deuteronomy, a later and more humane edition of early Hebrew law. Its clearest and best-known statement is, "It shall be life for life, eye for eye, tooth for tooth." It stresses equal vengeance, retaliation in kind and in similar measure. You are not entitled to do more to your enemy than he has done to you. By any manner of reckoning it represents a distinct advance over the earlier and more barbaric conception of unlimited vengeance. Here again it is far from being the conviction of only primitive men. We find it echoed widely among our own contemporaries.

For example, we are hearing an increasing number of our contemporaries justify the bombing of North and South Vietnam alike, even though civilian casualties are enormous, by simply saying, "This is war." Time and again we hear of villages in South Vietnam being completely leveled by a "mistake" on the part of some of our aircraft, or by design in order to create a free fire zone. Yet there will be no great sense of sin on our part because of this sort of thing. We take it for granted that such things will happen, and we say that until the enemy have been destroyed or have surrendered, the war must go on. Of course, we will regret such actions, but we will not repent of them to the extent of any serious effort to bring the war to an end now. We are all out to destroy the Viet Cong, we say. We are trying to protect the South Vietnamese civilians from "assassinations" by the

137

Viet Cong, we say. And so we will kill more people by our bombing raids than we ever claimed have been assassinated by the Viet Cong, and do this in order to wreak our vengeance upon the Viet Cong.

This is limited vengeance brought up to date. But not all of us will even want to limit our vengeance in these matters. Some of us will slip back to the lower rung and argue for unlimited vengeance and say with General LeMay that we ought to bomb North Vietnam back to the Stone Age. In fact, we have an increasing number of voices in our country asking that such be made our policy. By any manner of reckoning this is a regression as far back into barbarism as it is possible for human beings to go—yet we may go there. There is nothing to guarantee that we will struggle for the next higher rung in the biblical understanding of the meaning of forgiveness.

The third rung on that ladder is limited forgiveness, a relatively late arrival on the religious scene. Peter knew that forgiveness was a virtue, but he wanted to know how long he had to be governed by it. Consequently he became the spokesman for the best statement we have of limited forgiveness when he asked Jesus, "Lord, how often shall my brother sin against me, and I forgive him? As many as seven times?" Peter was taking the common sense position that there is a point beyond which it is not necessary to follow the ideal of forgiveness. Enough is enough! he would say. It is all right to be generous and forgiving up to a certain point, and then you have a right to defend yourself and exact your own justice and vengeance in order to bring the other fellow to his senses.

As we study the feelings clearly implicit in Peter's argument, we get the distinct impression that when Peter had reached the specified limit of forgiveness, he was then going to do what he had been wanting to do all the time! Before we pass too severe a judgment upon him for his shortsightedness, we ought to ask whether we would go even as far as he indicated a willingness to consider going. Most of us do well if we restrain our natural and normal desire to retaliate through one or more repetitions of an offense against us. Usually we do not have even that much fortitude.

Towering high above the ideal of limited forgiveness is the full Christian conception of unlimited forgiveness, the ideal and the goal of Christian ethics. It is to be found in Jesus' answer to Peter in the very incident we have been considering: "I do not say to you seven times, but seventy times seven"—the scriptural symbol of infinity. Nor is this an isolated statement of the principle. It underlies his admonition that we are to turn the other cheek, go the second mile, give our cloak as well if our coat is asked for. And let it be noted by those who think no one ever tried to live this way that he himself practiced what he preached when on the cross he prayed that most difficult of all prayers, "Father, forgive them; for they know not what they do."

Henry T. Hodgkin, a British writer, is well within the truth when he says that "Jesus . . . [places] over against the principle of mere limitation of retribution, namely, the principle of undeviating forgiveness."

III

Do you see any way of escaping the conclusion that Jesus' teaching on forgiveness and his actual act of forgiveness on the cross are of a piece with his understanding of God and God's will for man? I confess, I do not. There is a fine integrity between his faith in God's will and his deeds among men. Nor can I avoid the further implication that all this and more now come to me as a part of my Christian witness today. That, of course, is my deepest problem as a Christian these days. What I am about to say is both personal yet, I think, representative of at least some of you. As one who is always "standing in the need of prayer" and who is conscious of his many sins of omission and commission, I need and want to feel the power of the forgiving love of God. I need and want to feel that the mistakes I have made can be and have been overcome with his help. I need and want to feel the firm warmth of his love and purpose in my life and work.

The gospel of Jesus Christ invades my life with the assurance that all this is open to me, that God will actually help me if I will let him. The choice is mine. I need not let him help. I can reject him as I have done so many times in the past—more times than I can number—but he can help me only on his terms. I can and must choose whether I want him to help, but I have no choice whatever on how he shall help; that is the infinite difference between God and man, between creator and creature, between father and child.

Jesus makes it plain that only as I am willing to forgive others can God forgive me; that is the condition of forgiveness that I must confront. Only as I am willing to love others is it possible for his love for me to invade, empower, and direct my life. Was not this what Jesus said so beautifully in his prayer, "Forgive us our trespasses, as we forgive those who trespass against us"? Only as we forgive can we be forgiven. Only as we are willing to become the instruments of forgiveness can we ourselves experience the meaning of forgiveness.

Vital faith, then, is a channel through which the grace of God flows into, through, and beyond us into the lives of others. It is a channel, not a dammed up body of water that becomes as deadly to life as the Dead Sea is. Only as we are willing to become channels of the love of God can we know the saving power and grace of it ourselves. We must give it away in order to keep it. We must share it, or never know it.

The saints have always known this and have responded to it with great joy—perhaps that is why they are saints. Who but a saint could have fashioned this prayer from the texture of his experience:

> God be in my head,
>   And in my understanding;
> God be in mine eyes,
>   And in my looking;

God be in my mouth,
    And in my speaking;
God be in my heart,
    And in my thinking;
God be at mine end,
    And at my departing.

I cannot claim to be even close to sainthood and so must put this same faith in my own pedestrian way:

If God be love—as we believe,

If in Jesus Christ we have our clearest revelation of the will of God for the life of man—as we believe,

If we are co-workers together with God in the building of a kingdom of love on this earth—as we believe,

Then forgiveness is as essential as it is difficult.

It is a simple fact of history that the world has never been hospitable to the Christian ethic. No one knew this better than Jesus Christ. That is why he warned all who wanted to take him seriously to get rigged for battle with life as it is, with men as they are, and with the world as it is. He asked them to get ready not for a retreat from the world, but for an all-out assault on it. Not for him the caves by the Dead Sea—even then being used by men who despaired of the world. His faith led him into the marketplace, the temple, the village square, the judgment courts of Jew and Roman alike, and finally to Calvary.

Let us remember Jesus Christ! Especially when we are tempted to find the easy way, to measure the worth of the church by the amount of quiet she enjoys, the worth of our efforts by whether they get us a good press or are popular.

Let us remember Jesus Christ! Especially when we are tempted to hate anyone for any reason. For him and for us the only proper approach to injury, enmity, and injustice is the forgiving spirit which looks toward reconciliation. As we remember him, we will renounce the spirit of retaliation, root and branch! For as it is the will of God that we should live as a family of concerned, understanding human beings who love and trust each other, we must seek to bridge every chasm in the human family. And we must take the initiative by mastering and being mastered by the spirit of forgiveness as we find it in the love of God.

Hate closes doors between persons and peoples; forgiveness opens them. Hate depersonalizes human beings; it reduces them to ideologies or shadows that can be stuffed in one box and burned to a crisp by napalm bombs while we stand around and either applaud or say sadly, "Well, it's too bad, but . . . ." Forgiveness keeps persons alive as persons, as human beings, and insistently seeks the fullest possible personal relationship with them. Forgiveness never gives up on any person, no matter what he is or what he has done. He is and always will remain a child of God with whom we ought to be united in a spirit of understanding and brotherhood.

A recent writer has given us a story of the fighting between Germany and Russia in World War II. At the very height of the extreme bitterness which marked the feeling, as well as the fighting, a lull in the battle enabled some German soldiers to hear the moans of the wounded out ahead of their trench. One soldier volunteered to go out to see if he could help them and bring them back, if possible. He found a wounded man, a Russian, and brought him back crying, "He's a man! He's a man! He's like us! He's still alive!"

This is the discovery—so simple, so near at hand, yet so far off—that will end wars once and for all. Yet we can discover that men are men and must be treated with utmost concern and compassion only as we approach them in a spirit of forgiving love. And we do this not in a spirit of condescension, as though we were better than they, but because we are human as they are human and want to open and keep open the doors between us that will enable us to see and to have fellowship with each other.

Yet all this runs counter to what the world wants of us. Sometimes I find myself in fleeting moments wishing I had never taken that trip to South Vietnam in 1965 and met there some men and women of the Viet Cong; walked in the villages of the Mekong Delta that are now being destroyed by the fighting; seen people poking through the rubble of homes and villages destroyed by war, looking for some precious memento; been in the refugee camps around Saigon and seen their misery, unequaled anywhere; heard the roar of battle and seen the wounded coming back; heard the priests, Christian and Buddhist alike, tell of the hell in their villages in the war zones.

All this has simply unfitted me for using the symbols that are supposed to explain and justify what is going on in South Vietnam. Let the statesmen who dwell at ease in Washington and Hanoi explain that this is a war of national liberation or a war for freedom. I hear their words—thin, shallow, two-dimensional, self-righteous nouns, verbs, adjectives, and adverbs strung together and utterly unrelated to the lives of the people who are being assassinated by night and burned by napalm bombs by day. I hear what they say; I know that what they say is utterly irrelevant as far as the main issues are concerned, and yet I am supposed to be persuaded by what I hear.

We have lost contact with the humanness of the human beings involved in this war. When a Buddhist priest warns us that the war no longer has any meaning for the ordinary Vietnamese and that the deepest desire of the Vietnamese is to stay alive, we push it aside as nonsense and rush around putting up our own explanatory labels on events. We've lost the willingness to hear anyone but those who agree with us, who think well of us, who support us. We are dividing the world once more into two groups: we and they.

The Christian faith knows only one group: we. There are no "theys" to the Christian faith, and any attempt to create a "they" category for any other human being is a sin against the God of all men. That is why the spirit of forgiveness is essential to what we try to be and to do.

We must be able to see man if we are ever able to see God. If we cannot see man as man, we shall never

145

see God as God. And it is when we see God as God that we are truly able to see man as man, as a child of God.

There is in all this an awesome and wonderful circularity, a binding of the world together—man to man and God to man. And the spirit that opens this to us and us to this is that which comes through the words, "Father, forgive them; for they know not what they do."

10. He Suffered and Died

Scripture: *Mark 15:6-37*

I

Though the public ministry of Jesus of Nazareth lasted a very short time—not more than three years at most—it must have seemed an eternity to him. We may be sure that many times during it, especially during the latter part, his memory furnished him with what we call "flashbacks" of home and workshop in Nazareth and the thirty years he spent there. But once he had heard and accepted God's call to the public proclamation of the kingdom of God as it came to him by the Jordan River, he found himself in a canoe, as it were, on a mountain river, racing wildly through rapids with the noise of a Niagara coming from downstream.

What the Christian tradition has come to call "Holy Week" commemorates the last eight days of his life on earth, beginning with the triumphal entry into Jerusalem and ending with the incredible triumph of the Resurrection. Into that brief period of time are compressed the events which have produced more basic questions and answers than any other eight days in the whole history of human enterprise. Whereas John Reed carved out a kind of immortality in history with his book *Ten Days That Shook the World*, a vivid account of the beginning of the Communist revolution in Russia, the Four Gospels etched on the minds and souls of men eight days that not so much shook the world as gave all men the right to think of life and death in new terms—terms that made them think of a new life, a life that overleaped the limit of death itself. These eight days deal with the meaning of the suffering and death of Jesus of Nazareth.

As to the fact of his suffering and death there can be little doubt. We are well aware these days of the new book, *The Passover Plot*, by Hugh J. Schonfield, an English scholar of some standing among the experts. It is creating quite a stir with its thesis that while Jesus suffered, he did not die; that, in fact, his death on the cross was an illusion—"deception" is a better word—created by an elaborately arranged bit of simple fakery. Under the influence of the drugs which he had arranged to have put in his drink as he was on the cross, he became unconscious and appeared to be dead. He was then taken from the cross, put in a tomb, and later revived, to be greeted as one who had risen from the dead. So runs the thesis of Schonfield's book.

But I must say that all this smacks of the plot of a novel, much like the one Edgar A. Goodspeed once wrote. It was based on his specialty: New Testament manuscripts and the excitement of the search for new ones. But Dr. Goodspeed never mixed his judgment as a novelist with that of a New Testament scholar, as Schonfield seems to have done. It is simply incredible to think that so elaborate and crucial a plot could have convinced so many critical observers who could and would have readily checked the facts if they had had any doubt about it. We have little choice but to accept as substantially true the Gospel records of his suffering and death.

His suffering and death meant so much to the early church that the written Gospels probably began with the last week of his life and worked back to his ministry and childhood. That is where preachers like Peter and Paul began their preaching of the gospel, for in these events men found not alone the meaning of Jesus Christ, but the meaning of their own sufferings and death as well. They suffered with Christ even as he had suffered for them. As Paul said, "But if we have died with Christ, we believe that we shall also live with him."

II

Suffering is more than pain; pain of itself is not suffering. Suffering involves will, commitment, perseverance, and purpose blocked, thwarted, and apparently defeated by opposing forces. The suffering of Jesus Christ in this sense began at the moment when he was called of God into the public ministry, when that awesome word, "Thou art my beloved Son; with thee I am well pleased," fell like a mighty cleaver on his life, dividing it into two parts: before and after.

Then true suffering began in earnest. We would call it aloneness, estrangement, alienation. Or, as it was known then, he was set apart by God for the proclamation of the kingdom of God. The words to watch are "set apart." Whether we use ancient or modern names for it, his suffering began with his baptism. He stumbled into the nearby wilderness to try to sort out the full meaning of this event. What a struggle he had as he confronted his old world and its values with God's new world and its values! Status, security, power, wealth—all so important in the old world—gave way to one value: absolute obedience and complete trust in the will and love of God.

This was genuine suffering as well as genuine glory! It meant an irrevocable break with the only world he had known for thirty years. It meant the dangerous task of bringing that old world under the judgment of God's will for the world. It meant separation from and rejection by family, friends, neighbors, and fellow worshipers in synagogues and the temple.

We catch a glimpse of the realism of this rejection in Luke's terse account of what happened when he returned to Nazareth and tried to explain to his neighbors and friends what had happened to him and what he was trying to do: "When they heard this, all in the synagogue were filled with wrath. And they rose up and put him out of the city, and led him to the brow of the hill on which their city was built, that they might throw him down headlong. But passing through the midst of them he went away."

His family were so disturbed by rumors about him that they thought him out of his mind and actually tried to find him, bring him home, and persuade him to forget the mad vision. They found him speaking to a large crowd. They sent word that they wanted him to come home with them. He rejected them forthwith: " 'Who is my mother, and who are my brothers?' And stretching out his hand toward his disciples, he said, 'Here are my mother and my brothers! For whoever does the will of my Father in heaven is my brother, and sister, and mother.' " No more adequate symbol of separation could be found than that. And it must have cut him as deeply to say it as it did them to hear it.

But his sufferings were only begun with separation from home ties. Driven by loyalty to his call, he soon found himself in almost continuous conflict, or at least open misunderstanding, with the religious leaders of his people, the very ones at whose feet he had sat for instruction all his life. When he appealed to them in the name of God, they quoted the Law in reply. When he appealed to them in the name of man, they quoted the Law in reply. When he appealed to them in the name of mercy and forgiveness, they quoted the Law in reply.

When he appealed to them in the name of the kingdom of God, they quoted the Law in reply.

This break, early discernible, rapidly became a tremendous chasm. He was aware of it, and the realization of it must have cut him to the quick, good and faithful Jew that he was. For it carried with it the certainty that he would become a hated, hunted, feared, and most unwelcome person in places hitherto so dear to him: the synagogue, the temple, and Jerusalem itself. He could not hold back his tears for Jerusalem as he approached it for the last time: "O Jerusalem, Jerusalem, killing the prophets and stoning those who are sent to you! How often would I have gathered your children together as a hen gathers her brood under her wings, and you would not. Behold, your house is forsaken and desolate."

Though he wept over Jerusalem, there is no record that Jerusalem wept over him—at least not then. For when he entered the city, the instant of triumph he enjoyed on Palm Sunday proved to be a false dawn that was rapidly swallowed by an even blacker night.

The suffering that may well have hurt almost as much as separation from family was his inability to get certain essentials of the gospel over to his disciples. With three years of his fellowship and teaching behind them some of them quarreled openly on the final trip to Jerusalem as to who was to sit in the seats of honor in the kingdom! Later when he asked them to watch and pray, they went to sleep. He must have wondered whether his confidence in them had been misplaced.

This sense of alienation from man cut so deeply that it threatened to destroy the vision itself as the last days closed in upon him. That is why in the garden this prayer was wrenched from his agony: "Father, if thou art willing, remove this cup from me; nevertheless not my will, but thine, be done."

A special kind of suffering reserved for the choicest human spirits ran through his entire ministry—the death of a dream, the dimming down of high hopes. The ministry had begun so well, with crowds, acclaim, men leaving all and following him. For a brief period it must have seemed that the great new age was actually opening in glory. But not for long did this high hope remain in his sky! Down it came, and with it "the dark night of the soul" was upon him. And the blackest part of that night came during the last week of his life.

We are, I fear, almost too familiar with the actual sufferings he endured during that week. Do we really feel the keen edge of all that happened to him: sleeplessness, fatigue, the crown of thorns, the hard blows of rough men, the flogging, the bleeding, sheer exhaustion from carrying a one-hundred-pound cross for at least half a mile? Thank God, Simon of Cyrene was there to lift the cross when it crushed him to the road. Then came the suffering on the cross itself and slow death to the obbligato of jeers and howls all around.

Once more aloneness threatened: "My God, my God, why hast thou forsaken me?" And the healing answer must have sped from the hearing Father to the listening Son: "Father into thy hands I commit my spirit!"

III

What, we must now ask ourselves, did all this mean? to him? to his enemies? to the disciples? and, praying God's forgiveness for the impertinence of it, to God himself?

This long pattern of suffering undoubtedly meant more to Jesus Christ than we can ever know. But we may be sure that it meant the testing of his vision and call. It plunged him into conflict, doubt, and despair. Yet in those very depths his suffering confirmed the worth of his vision and gave him the strength to live and die for it.

He came to terms with suffering—and so must we. We learn through suffering, as a distinguished German philosopher, Nicolai Hartmann, has pointed out. Suffering, he writes, is one of the great values of life. It is "an actual liberation, an awakening of a deeper moral power . . . whoever has been tested in suffering is tempered steel—for him nothing is too difficult . . . he is . . . raised to a higher moral power." [1] The purchase price of suffering is well worth all that it costs. Suffering changes our attitude toward life and changes it for the better; suffering sees below the surface of life; it peers into the depths; it enables us to see things hitherto hidden from us.

Only one who has been laid on the anvil of life and pounded, pounded, pounded, can know the agony of the blows that fall on all men sooner or later. Only one

[1] *Ethics* (New York: Humanities Press, 1966), II, 140-41.

who has endured the suffering of separation can feel the loneliness that tears at the roots of our self-confidence. Only one who has worn a crown of thorns can feel the menace of ultimate despair that all men of vision feel. An ancient Christian maxim puts it in an unforgettable way: "Who does not carry his cross is not my brother."

Strange as it may sound to put it this way, we may be certain that given the choice on Black Friday, our Lord would not have exchanged the cross for the carpenter shop. For the way that led to that cross had led him home, quite literally—home to man and home to God.

What did his suffering and death mean to his enemies, the ones who schemed and plotted and finally had him helpless in their hands? For the religious leaders it meant victory, pure and simple: the triumph of righteousness; the protection of the faith of the fathers from contamination; the vindication of a heritage in the face of an irresponsible challenge.

For the Roman it meant the end of one more potential, if not actual, troublemaker and subversive; one more number added to the long list of men crucified as warning and threat to anyone who might get ideas about changing things.

What did his suffering and death mean to his disciples, to the ones closest to him who had heard but brushed aside his warning of the Niagara ahead of them? To Judas his suffering meant complete disillusionment and good enough reason for betraying him. What did it mean to the eleven who remained? Disbelief, bewilder-

155

ment, and despair. Had the cross ended it all, really ended it, what would the disciples have done? Would they have gone back home as soon as sabbath law permitted them to travel and tried to forget it? At first glance yes, but only at first glance! There was more to their faith than that! He had gotten through to them. Their association with him had so completely transformed their lives that they were ready for the great commission to go to the ends of the earth with the gospel. Deep within them something was waiting for his word to surface and take over. They too had suffered alongside him for three years. They too had had their eyes and spirits opened to the hidden depths of life. He had yoked their lives to each other, to himself, and to God in so firm a fashion that they came to be known as "the pillars" in the early church. They were hailed as those "who had been with Jesus," those who had shared in his sufferings, as well as his glory.

What did his suffering and death mean to God, if we may be so presumptuous as to ask the question? There is only one place to look for our answer: in history, in what God has done through Jesus Christ. That and that alone tells us what those three years must have meant to God.

I've always been interested in the fact that while our fathers were able to reach substantial, if temporary, agreement on doctrines and dogmas about many things, they were never able to fashion one that would explain the sufferings and death of Jesus Christ. They tried it

—they could not help trying it—but no one explanation ever won enough general acceptance to become an official doctrine. But official or not, the faith that man has been saved by what was done in Jesus Christ has become a part of our hymns, our prayers, our sacraments, and our day-to-day faith.

One of the first songs I recall hearing sung is "The Old Rugged Cross"; it was sung by my mother as she, daughter of a preacher, went about her work in our farm home. As I grew up, I was taught to sing "When I Survey the Wondrous Cross," "In the Cross of Christ I Glory," and many other testaments of faith.

In the Communion service on Holy Thursday we commemorate the Last Supper our Lord had with his disciples, and pray: "Almighty God, our heavenly Father, who of thy tender mercy didst give thine only son Jesus Christ to suffer death upon the cross for our redemption; who made there, by the one offering of himself, a full, perfect, and sufficient sacrifice for the sins of the whole world; and did institute, and in his holy Gospel command us to continue, a perpetual memory of his precious death until his coming again:

"Hear us, O merciful Father, we most humbly beseech thee, . . ."

IV

The Christians whom we meet in the New Testament might differ on many details of faith but never on the

157

principle of it. With Paul they determined to remember one thing and one thing only as they went to the ends of the earth: Jesus Christ and him crucified. They understood that in his suffering and death there was something far more than an ordinary tragedy of an innocent man being put to a cruel death by evil or careless men.

But what more there was in it than that a critical world has demanded to know. "God was in Christ reconciling the world to himself," Paul answered. Christ "bore our sins on the tree," another answered. "He suffered there for me," "He gave himself for me," we say and sing. "Who made . . . of himself, a full, perfect, and sufficient sacrifice for the sins of the whole world," we say in our service of Holy Communion.

While such hallowed sentiments may be enough for some of us who have been reared in a Christian environment, the keenly skeptical outside world has demanded a more careful statement of the meaning of the suffering and death of Jesus Christ. And Christian thinkers over nineteen hundred years have done what Christian thinkers must always do, namely try to give a reason for the hope that is within them. Their efforts to interpret the basic meaning of the events we have been studying are gathered up in one word some of us have heard from childhood but possibly some of us have not heard at all: *atonement*—the work of God in Christ.

If time permitted us to look carefully at the major interpretations of atonement, we would understand many of the phrases in our hymns and prayers that sound strange in modern ears:

O Love divine, what hast Thou done!
The incarnate God hath died for me!
The Father's co-eternal Son
Bore all my sins upon the tree!
The Son of God for me hath died:
My Lord, my Love, is crucified.

But we need not lose ourselves in a forest of conflicting theories as to what the cross means. Let us settle on the one fact on which there is unbroken agreement: in Christ on the cross we see someone more, and even other, than a teacher of great truths; we see the love of God incarnate in human life. We see the truths of God come alive in our life on this earth, being doubted, derided, shouted down, rejected, in the person of Jesus Christ. But there is no sense of defeat as we study that cross; only the glory and the victory of it come through. We are grasped by the power of the love of God. We are seized by a purpose not ours for life. The cross is God in action making his ultimate effort to break through to the hearts and minds of men like us and claim us for his own.

For in Christ on the cross we see the perfect and final revelation of the love of God for man, in and through which we are led to a new life of love for man and God. Not that evil is forgotten or denied. It is overcome! For in the cross we see the keen awareness of our estrangement from God through the blindness of sin and self-will. Separated from God, we are lost in sin, in the darkness of selfish passion and power, in the night of

159

loneliness and despair, groping our way toward a kind of spiritual death that dooms life to extinction.

The cross changed all this. There God reached us as he had never been able to reach men before. There God inserted himself in human life and history in such fashion that he spoke from within the human situation to human beings like us. Nor did he speak by marvelous precepts alone, though they are there. He spoke by his life. For Jesus Christ was the Word of God incarnate, we say. When men heard him, they heard as for the first time the love of God confronting them, telling them, showing them a way out of the human predicament, revealing a way of living with man and with God that would give life eternal purpose and meaning. Nor could even the fury of human sin which sought to silence the divine Word on the cross silence or defeat God's purpose. For that cross served to trumpet to the world the love of God; the word of that cross invades every nook and cranny of human life, letting men know the way, the truth, and the life. When we say we accept Jesus Christ and him crucified, we mean simply that we follow by faith the clear meaning of the love of God which we find in him. And we do so, confident that this will break the spell of sin and drive away the fear of death, for the love of God is eternal, all-powerful, and all-merciful.

V

Is it possible to put this in a way that speaks to the need of our time? I do not know, but I do know that we must try. I cannot speak for others, but for me it comes down to something as elemental as this:

I feel in this New Testament record of the sufferings and death of Jesus Christ the full power of the evil we do to each other, especially to those who feel "set apart" by God for a special witness. I see Paul and Peter dying on their crosses, Savonarola and Servetus perishing in the flames, Luther with a price on his head, Wesley ostracized by the church of his fathers, and the heresy trials past and present. I think of the cruelty of man to man that we accept or ignore or, worst of all, get accustomed to until it is possible for six million of us to perish in furnaces and fifty million to be killed in war, and the rest of us pass it by with little more than a slight shrug of horror.

I see in the cross a symbol of the costliness of obedience to the will of God in this world, where things like this happen. Shocked as I always am when I try to find my way to the foot of his cross, I am stunned by the realization that there are so many empty hills and waiting crosses for those among us who dare to be different for God's sake. Let no man think that the final crucifixion has yet occurred on the face of this earth!

I discover too that secret and ample reservoirs of strength are open to all men who will obey God. The man who is a rebel for God's sake has bread to eat that we know not of; he is buoyed up by a joy that baffles pedestrian worldlings like the rest of us.

The longer I study it, the more the cross comes to

mean this to me: in Jesus Christ, God identified himself with man in an unforgettable and inseparable way. God knows what it is like to be a man living on this earth. God has stood where we stand. He knows what we are up against, and he will stand at our side if we will let him. Not for me any of this talk about God and man separated by "an infinite chasm"! Not with the cross meaning what it does.

The cross makes crystal-clear just how real and powerful the love of God is. When we seek to be related to it, or to give ourselves to it, we are seeking a relationship with the most powerful force on earth. The love of God is powerful enough to enter into and transform our most evil deeds. It can make a crown of thorns into a priceless diadem; it can make a cruel instrument of torture into a glorious symbol of God's true intention for all men.

The scope of human suffering has not noticeably diminished since Jesus lived and died, but our capacity to meet and master it has been enlarged beyond all measure. We sorrow for loved ones who are gone, but we no longer sorrow as those who have no hope.

When one of the boys who grew up playing with our sons lost his son this summer, he wrote brokenheartedly, "This thing has put our faith to the ultimate test. I'm confused as to just what to believe. Understanding a Creator that tolerates such suffering of an innocent child is difficult to say the least." How many millions of parents have felt just as this young father felt? How many in this and every other country now at war feel that way now? Only God knows, for only he can hear or bear to hear their cries. It is not to still the anguish of the loss, but it is to unlock the reservoirs of strength to repeat the old, old story of the bereaved mother who asked the minister, "Where was your God when my son was killed?" And he replied, "Just where he was when his son was killed."

In Jesus Christ the love of God comes alive and walks up and down on this earth among people like us, seeking entrance into lives and homes like ours. In him we see the glory and feel the power of that love, and we know that it will overcome and transform the world if it can find utterance, expression, and incarnation in persons like us. That is the gospel we preach, and preach it we must by lip and life to the very end of our lives. For the great commission continues to hold: to go to the ends of the earth and preach the gospel to every creature.

11. He Lives Eternally

Scripture: *Luke 23:13-37*

I

Doubts about the physical resurrection of Jesus Christ have plagued Christians from the time of the alleged event until our own day. And I must make immediate confession that we have not yet fashioned so sharp a spear of fact and logic as to finally slay all of the dragons of doubt on this matter.

We have been fighting those dragons a long time: the Gospel of Matthew records the first of these encounters. This Gospel, written approximately forty years after the earthly life of Jesus, tells us that even then skeptics were circulating the story that the disciples of Jesus had stolen his body from the tomb and used the empty tomb as proof of his resurrection. One of the latest encounters occurred with the appearance of Hugh Schonfield's book *The Passover Plot.*

Looking at the facts we have in the New Testament, we discover the unqualified and unanimous conviction of the early Christians that Jesus Christ had overcome death in some wonderfully divine way and continued to live and reign over them. Nowhere do they refer to him in the past tense, as someone who had once lived as did Socrates or David. Past, present, and future tense are all rolled up in one bundle of time as they speak of him. He is "the same yesterday and today and for ever."

Paul's letters are full of references to him and always as a living power and presence—as real to Paul as were his companions, Timothy, Mark, and Luke.

The Four Gospels present Jesus as a living person. The rest of the New Testament is a record of men's reaction to his continuing presence and power as the Lord of their lives. The Christian church then and now is centered in him as the Lord of the church as well as of the lives of all who believe in him and are in the church.

That is why our interpretation of the deeds of Christ must include his triumph over death. For this deed caused the ancient Christian shout of joy: "He lives eternally!"

We must resist the desire simply to celebrate this as a fact, for today many Christians are honestly confused about it. For some of us it is not a fact. For others it is so clouded in mystery as to be more confusing than helpful. What do we mean when we say that this person who was born about 6 B.C. and was put to death in A.D. 28 or 29 lives eternally? That he lived then—yes; but now? What do we mean by that?

II

The New Testament, of course, faces these questions and suggests answers that are quite simple. For the New Testament writers he lived in two dimensions, as it were: as a remembered person and as a present power.

His disciples remembered him, and they passed their memories on to the early church in the Gospels. The disciples themselves were idolized in the early church because they had been with Jesus. Wherever Peter went on his missionary travels, he was plied with questions about Jesus Christ. The other disciples were held in equally high esteem. The earliest Christian community recognized them as authorities because they had known Jesus Christ during his public ministry. There is reason to believe that the Gospel of Mark is based on the reminiscences of Peter as written by John Mark, who traveled with the aging disciple as interpreter and companion. There is also reason to think that the Gospel of Matthew has as its heart not alone the record of Mark, but also 150 sayings of Jesus that were jotted down by the disciple Matthew himself. There is also reason to think that Luke, who spent two years in or around Jerusalem while Paul was in prison in Caesarea, gathered all of the stories he could from those who had known Jesus Christ and included them along with the record of Mark in the Gospel that bears his name.

I mention these facts because it is necessary to keep in mind the solid foundation of firsthand information that in some way or other underlies our knowledge of Jesus Christ. We are not making up stories about someone who never lived. The early Christian community gathered first around him, then around those who had known him, and finally around the New Testament, which was the record of his life and their understanding of what he meant.

Jesus Christ, then, from the very beginning of our tradition was remembered as a teacher, a leader, a prophet, and, above all, as one sent of God to break the power of sin and death and to inaugurate the kingdom of God on earth.

But the early church was not a memorial society gathered around a dead hero. It was a church, a called and commissioned community. Each one in that church felt personally called "out of the world" by Christ and commissioned by him to take the gospel to the ends of the earth. Jesus was a present power as well as a remembered person. He was thought of as the actual head of the church, as the vine of which they were the branches, as the shepherd with them as his sheep, as the elder brother with whom they were to work in the service of God.

He has continued to live in many ways in the Christian tradition. Obviously, he lives in the New Testament. As long as the Bible is read and cherished, men will know of him and of what he meant to those who put the records in the form in which we have them.

He lives in the church that bears his name. It is far too easy to spend so much time lamenting the things

167

that separate Christians into four hundred varieties of churches that we neglect the one thing that unites us— Jesus Christ as the Lord of life. There is no shadow of disagreement among us on this. In fact, our unity in him is the biggest reason why it is both possible and necessary for the separate churches to draw together as they are doing in the ecumenical movements today. He spans all our differences. That is why we feel at home in services of worship in churches other than our own. He is why I am able to feel at home whether in an Orthodox or Roman Catholic or Baptist church in Moscow or Kiev or wherever I have found myself in recent trips to Russia.

Jesus Christ lives in the theology of the church. He lives in our ethics and disturbs us no end there. He lives in the two sacraments of our church: baptism and Holy Communion. We baptize our children in his name and dedicate them to growth in his service. In the Communion service we speak of the Lord's table, as indeed we hope it is. He lives in the many arts that bless the church. The hymns and anthems are centered in him. Our prayers are in his spirit and in his name.

He lives in our hopes, dreams, life, and work. We are not our own; we are his. The church is not ours; it is his, and we are blessed beyond our deserts by being privileged to share and to serve in it. We go to church, hopefully, to worship the God whom we find in him. There we take our children for baptism, for instruction in the faith. There an increasing number of adults go to learn of his meaning for and claim on their lives. There we go to pray for guidance, to search for light and strength for living. There we take our dead for the final rites of this earthly span of life, trusting to him the continuing care of their spirits. In those dark moments we cry with Paul: "I know whom I have believed and I am sure that he is able to guard until that Day what has been entrusted to me."

III

Jesus Christ lives in the men and women whom he has inspired and who in turn have enriched our lives. Each one of us could draw up his own list of such persons. Some would be ancient and some contemporary. Yet let us never forget that for everyone we are able to call by name there will be ten thousand others to whom we are equally indebted, but whose names we do not know. They live and he lives in what we call the Christian tradition, which for two thousand years has been a very real force in shaping our lives.

In saying this I am not now thinking of biographies I have read, but rather of persons I have known. For it is human beings very much like ourselves who make him come alive on the level of believable common life.

Bishop Arthur J. Moore of The Methodist Church was fond of telling a story of something that happened in a church in Georgia. A girl in the town had fallen in love with and married a man who had come into the community. In due time they were expecting a child. Suddenly her world disintegrated. Her husband left, confessing that he had a wife and family elsewhere. The baby was born and the young mother was determined to have him baptized in the church. As she came forward with him, twelve deacons of the church came and surrounded her and the child and shared the vows to bring up the child in the faith.

In the Mount Vernon Place Church of Baltimore I had an understanding with some of the key men and women that whenever someone needed them, I would call on them, and they never let me or the one in need down—not once.

I recall the wonderful old churchman, a storekeeper in our little town, whom I, a callow youth of seventeen and just entering the ministry, once asked, "What is the most wonderful thing that ever happened to you?" He answered, "To know and serve Jesus Christ and to share my life with those he has given to me."

Churchmen—ministers and laymen alike—fail; we know that. We fail many times, but not always. When I hear cynics downgrading the church and trying to write off churchmen as pious frauds and hypocrites on parade, I remember persons like these and say of them what was said of the old minister in James M. Barrie's book *The Little Minister*, "Such men are the strong nails that hold the world together." Yet, I cannot separate such men from the One who inspired their lives and from whom they lighted the torch of their faith and convictions.

When I find myself wondering whether I am setting too much stock in incidents like these, I am strengthened

by the judgments of great men of letters like Arnold
Toynbee and Sholem Asch.

When Arnold Toynbee was completing his six-volume
study of history, he was summing up the results of many
of the great leaders in the human enterprise. He had
listed them all carefully: the militarists, the kings, the
philosophers, and finally the human and divine saviors,
and the gods. He concluded, "At the final ordeal of
death, few, even of these would-be saviour gods, have
dared to put their title to the test by plunging into the
icy river. And now, as we stand and gaze with our eyes
fixed upon the farther shore, a single figure rises from
the flood and straightway fills the whole horizon. There
is the Saviour. . . ." [1]

Sholem Asch, a great Jewish writer of our time, gave
us three powerful historical novels; one about Mary,
another about Jesus Christ, and a third about Paul. But
his book *One Destiny* [2] lifts what I have been saying
about the power of Jesus Christ from the warmly personal experiences I have mentioned to the level of a uni-
versal human experience.

A little less than two thousand years ago, there came into
our world among the Jewish people and to it a personage
who gave substance to the illusion perceived by our fathers
in their dream. Just as water fills up the hollowness of the

[1] *A Study of History* (New York: Oxford University Press, 1935-61), VI, 278.
[2] Milton Hundus, trans. (New York: G. P. Putnam's Sons, 1945).
© 1945 Sholem Asch. Used by permission of the authorized representatives of the estate of Sholem Asch.

171

ocean, so did he fill the empty world with the spirit of the one living God. No one before him and no one after him has bound our world with the fetters of law, of justice, and of love, and brought it to the feet of the one living almighty God as effectively as did this personage who came to an Israelite house in Nazareth of Galilee—and this he did not by the might of the sword, or fire and steel, like the law-givers of other nations, but by the power of his mighty spirit and of his teachings. He, as no one else before him, raised our world from "the void and nothingness" in which it kept losing its way and bound it with strong ties of faith to the known goal, the pre-determined commandment of an almighty throne so as to become a part of the great, complete, everlasting scheme of things. He, as no other, raised man from his probationary state as a beast, from his dumb, blind, and senseless existence, gave him a goal and a purpose and made him a part of the divine. He, as no other, stands before our eyes as an example and a warning—both in his divine form and in his human one—and demands of us, harries us, prods us to follow his example and carry out his teachings. No one but he sheds about himself such an aura of moral power, which, with a divine touch, has molded our world and our character; and no one's strength but his own has reached into our time, being the most potent influence in our everyday lives, inspiring us to goodness and exalted things, being the measure and scale of our deeds at every hour and every minute.

I cannot think of any passage outside the New Testament which provides a more vivid portrayal of the present power of Jesus Christ as a living force and fact in history.

IV

But quotations from the great men of the world stop one step short of where we live. Finally, each man must make answer for himself: Is Jesus Christ living or dead as far as we are concerned? Is he a historical person remembered in scripture, the church, and pious art, and nothing more as far as we know personally? When we remind ourselves of what he did, we do not wonder that men like Toynbee and Asch—one a Christian, the other a Jew—write of him as they did. Nor can we escape the real challenge of trying to identify ourselves with him or against him as a living fact. What in essence did he do that makes him a living force in our lives today?

I must give my own answer to that, and I do so gladly. To put it in a sentence: he revealed to us the truth of God—that God is love; that this world was created in love, is sustained by love, and is redeemed by love. What God does is purposed in love; what he wills is rooted and grounded in love. That is why the only possible human response to God must be in kind. Jesus put God's ultimate will for human beings very simply in the great commandment: to love God with all our heart, soul, mind, and strength and our neighbor as ourselves. So far from being hopeless, helpless idealism, this commandment is the only hopeful, powerful way for men to live—if God be love.

Christian mystics from Tersteegen to Rufus Jones have been praying, "Let thy love fall as fire from heaven upon the altar of our hearts." Christian thinkers from

Origen to Whitehead have seized our Lord's momentous revelation of the nature of God and used it as the key to unlock the mysteries of this universe. Men like Augustine and Walter Rauschenbusch have found—and we can find—that to love God is to love truth, beauty, and goodness and that to enlist in the service of God is to seek the fullest possible meaning of these great values for human beings and human life. Christian prophets from St. Francis of Assisi to A. J. Muste have known that to love God, the God whom we find in Jesus Christ, is to carry the rewards and rebukes of the world lightly and to value only the presence of the holy. And humble persons like ourselves who neither lay claim to greatness nor think much about it have found in the love revealed to us in Jesus Christ the light we need for walking through dark days, the strength we need to keep in and keep at the tasks of daily life no matter how hard they are.

Why is it that those who name the name of Jesus Christ, who enlist in his service, who seek to find their purpose for living in his understanding of the purpose of God—why, I ask you and I ask myself, is it we will not give up the hopeless struggle for a world of brotherhood, justice, peace, and love? We do not, we will not quit because we cannot without full surrender of him, of his vision of God and man and of that kingdom of love in which all men live as brothers one of another and as sons of God. To give up the struggle for this kind of world is to give up our faith in Jesus Christ and to cut off our consciousness of his living presence and sustaining strength.

George Tyrrell's answer for himself is answer for all: "Again and again I have been tempted to give up the struggle, but always the figure of that strange man hanging on his cross sends me back to my work again."

Jesus himself anticipated the way in which he would live eternally, and it was not on clouds of glory as our painters have so often portrayed him. "Where two or three are gathered in my name, there am I in the midst of them." Or as John put it in Revelation, "Behold, I stand at the door and knock; if anyone hears my voice and opens the door, I will come in to him and eat with him, and he with me."

It is as simple as that, if that is simple; meet in his name, in loyalty to him, with a will to serve the God of love in human life and to do this in the physical and moral wastelands of the modern world.

To experience the living Christ is as simple as wanting the spirit of love to be the spirit of our lives, our homes, our relationships—and making the effort to let it be so, for as we do, he enters in and becomes a part of our lives. As we do this, we like the two men on the road to Emmaus will discover that the simplest things, like the breaking of bread, enable us to see him as he really is.

Does this sort of thought compromise his lordship or cancel the mystery and the meaning of it all? I think not. The most wonderful and mysterious things in the world are the simplest ones. Love for one another, compassion for one another, joy in one another, life and work shared with one another—these are simple enough, yet the deepest meanings in this universe find tongue in and through them. Only as we find the true meaning of Jesus Christ in them, in the simple things, have we anything at all to say about the larger issues and larger problems of the world. The converse of this is true: as we do find him in Christian fellowship, we find something that we must either say in terms of the larger issues or lose it from our lives.

Jesus lives eternally, in the songs of little children, in the proclamations of faith of mature men, in the prayers of all of us as we seek to find our way through the doors of tomorrow.

Our granddaughter, six years of age, returned from Sunday school one day last fall singing with great gusto, "Jesus Loves Me." Her father asked, "Do you think Jesus really loves you?" She stopped singing and said, "He doesn't even know me!" But as she grows older, she will learn as we all do that he does know us and that we can know him better than any of us ever do.

To know him is to know God; to know him is to know man; to know him is to know the true meaning of life and death. And as we know him, all things fall into a kind of pattern and purpose that gives life a radiance of meaning that can only be called holy. That, I believe, is where Jesus Christ really lives eternally—in the holiness of life, of work, of human relationships. He is the Lord of life—life today, tomorrow, and forevermore.

176

HAROLD A. BOSLEY

Since 1962 HAROLD A. BOSLEY has served as senior minister of Christ Church (United Methodist) in New York City.

For over thirty years Dr. Bosley has been in great demand as a lecturer at seminaries, colleges, universities, and pastors' schools throughout the country. His personal ministry has taken him to seminaries in Japan and Korea and has included participation in assemblies of the World Council of Churches and interfaith missions in South Vietnam and Russia.

His writing ministry has resulted in more than thirteen books, several contributions to commentaries and encyclopedias, and articles in a wide range of religious periodicals. Frequent radio and television appearances are also a part of his active schedule.

Prior to 1962 Dr. Bosley was minister at First Methodist Church in Evanston, Illinois, Dean of the Divinity School at Duke University, and pastor of Mount Vernon Place Methodist Church in Baltimore.